The Success
Case Method

The Success Case Method

Find Out Quickly What's Working and What's Not

Robert O. Brinkerhoff

BK

BERRETT-KOEHLER PUBLISHERS, INC.
San Francisco

Berrett-Koehler Publishers, Inc.
235 Montgomery Street, Suite 650
San Francisco, CA 94104-2916
Tel: (415) 288-0260   Fax: (415) 362-2512   www.bkconnection.com

Ordering Information

Quantity sales. Special discounts are available on quantity purchases by corporations, associations, and others. For details, contact the "Special Sales Department" at the Berrett-Koehler address above.

Individual sales. Berrett-Koehler publications are available through most bookstores. They can also be ordered direct from Berrett-Koehler: Tel: (800) 929-2929; Fax: (802) 864-7626; www.bkconnection.com

Orders for college textbook/course adoption use. Please contact Berrett-Koehler: Tel: (800) 929-2929; Fax: (802) 864-7626.

Orders by U.S. trade bookstores and wholesalers. Please contact Publishers Group West, 1700 Fourth Street, Berkeley, CA 94710. Tel: (510) 528-1444; Fax (510) 528-3444.

Berrett-Koehler and the BK logo are registered trademarks of Berrett-Koehler Publishers, Inc.

Printed in the United States of America

Berrett-Koehler books are printed on long-lasting acid-free paper. When it is available, we choose paper that has been manufactured by environmentally responsible processes. These may include using trees grown in sustainable forests, incorporating recycled paper, minimizing chlorine in bleaching, or recycling the energy produced at the paper mill.

Library of Congress Cataloging-in-Publication Data

Brinkerhoff, Robert O.
    The success case method : find out quickly what's working and what's not / by Robert O. Brinkerhoff.
       p. cm.
    Includes bibliographical references and index.
    ISBN 1-57675-185-6
       1. Success in business—Research—Methodlology. 2. Business failures—Research—Methodology. 3. Case method. I. Title.

HF5386.5.B837 2002
658'.7'22—dc21   2002028007

First Edition
07 06 05 04 03 02   10 9 8 7 6 5 4 3 2 1

Contents

Preface

Managers, executives, consultants, and other leaders from all organizational walks of life are continuously vexed by the challenge of making change work. Each year, organizations spend millions upon millions of dollars trying out new innovations and improvements, from new tools and technology to new techniques, training, and organizational schemes. Inevitably, some of these new things work quite well and others don't. In fact, it is almost always true that none of these many changes works completely. Some users of new tools and methods will get marvelous results, while others using the same tools will experience frustration and failure. To mangle P. T. Barnum, you can get some things to work with some of the people some of the time, but you can never get everything to work with everyone all of the time.

Change leaders need good information to guide change. When things are working well, they must notice them and nurture even better results. When things are not working, they must notice and fix them. Without good information, change leaders are flying blind. With good information, they can help organizations and the people in them experience the greatest success possible and get the greatest returns for their change investments.

The Success Case Method is a carefully crafted, simple, and proven way of quickly finding out how well a new organizational initiative is working. Using the Success Case Method, people can get useful and accurate information about new initiatives: What results are being achieved using new approaches, what is working, what is not, and how it can be improved. The methods and tools described in this book can help change leaders, executives, managers, consultants, training directors, and anyone else who is trying to get things to work better.

Evaluation, of course, is the general methodology that is available for finding out how well things are working, but rarely do change leaders have sufficient time or money for full-blown evaluation studies. On the other hand, they need better information than casual hearsay evidence and gut reactions can give them. The Success Case Method is a fresh in-between alternative that has reasonable rigor and accuracy but is relatively cheap and quick, and produces credible evidence about what is working and what is not in a way people—from senior executives to production supervisors—find believable, compelling, and useful.

In today's world, things are moving faster than ever before, and the ability to get organizations to perform more effectively is especially crucial. Change is an inevitable and necessary ingredient for effectiveness, and those who guide it most constructively will prevail. The Success Case Method is not a cure-all for managing change, but it is a powerful and helpful tool for helping change leaders do their job more effectively.

Here are some of the problems and scenarios a Success Case Method (SCM) inquiry can help address:

A new product launch is faltering. Some sales representatives have been very successful in selling a new product, but most are struggling and sales performance is not where it was hoped to be. What are these few successful reps doing, and how can we use their experience to make this new product launch successful?

Nobody believes new welfare practices are really helping single mothers. Many caseworkers are discouraged about what they see as harsh new requirements, but some families seem to be getting useful help. What is really happening, and how can we accurately evaluate the new approach?

Why are some managers losing staff, but others retain theirs? Some managers are clearly successful in establishing positive relationships, and retention is not a problem. But many others are struggling. What are the good ones doing that the bad ones are not, and vice versa? How can we help them all be successful?

Senior management is demanding proof. A new and controversial training program has drawn a lot of attention. Some people swear it is working, but there are a lot of skeptics. How can we quickly, but credibly and accurately, demonstrate the good results we think it is achieving in a way that senior management will believe?

Is a pilot program ready to launch company-wide? Is the new program getting the results expected? What should be changed to assure the success of a broad rollout?

Frustrated new technology users are swamping the help desk A lot of people are having a hard time with some new technology, but a few seem to be able to make it work. What are these few doing? How can their success be spread to others?

A reorganization into branch offices isn't working consistently. Some branches have been immediately successful and employees are happy, but others are not working well at all, and employees are starting to look elsewhere. What can be done to learn from success and turn around faltering branches?

These are representative of some of the problems and venues in which the SCM has proven to be helpful. Many evaluation approaches lead to overall "thumbs up or down" judgments, thus the few successes a program may be having get thrown out in the general bathwater of a larger initiative that is not working well. But, because the SCM looks for success, no matter how small or infrequent, it helps new initiatives grow and become more successful.

Specifically, the SCM gets information to help address four key questions about a new change initiative:

1. *What is really happening?* Who's using what, and how well? Who's not using things as planned? What's getting used, and what isn't? Which people and how many are having success? Which people and how many are not?

2. *What results are being achieved?* What good, if any, is being realized? What goals are being met? What goals are not? Is the change delivering the promised and hoped for results? What unintended results are happening?

3. *What is the value of the results?* What sort of dollar or other value can be placed on the results? Does the program appear to be worthwhile? Is it producing results worth more than its costs?

What is its return on investment? How much more value could it produce if it were working better?

4. *How can it be improved?* What's helping? What's getting in the way? What could be done to get more people to use it? How can everyone be more like those few who are most successful?

Brief Success Case studies can be planned and implemented roughly and quickly, showing credible and valid results in as little as one or two weeks. On the other hand, the Success Case Method can be employed in a more thorough fashion, including defensible estimates of return on investment (ROI), and otherwise substituting for a more complete evaluation study. Importantly, the Success Case Method is especially useful for assessing "soft skill," social, and other subtle outcomes and impacts that are usually thought of as hard to measure.

The Success Case Method is based on the ancient craft of storytelling. We all know that stories are powerful because they tap deep emotions and compel interest. But stories can also raise doubts about their truthfulness and validity—how do we know it's not "just a story?". The Success Case Method employs stories, but it combines storytelling with rigorous—albeit balanced and practical—evaluation methods and principles to combine the credibility of scientific findings with the emotional impact of stories. The stories produced by the SCM cite solid evidence—evidence that would "stand up in court" and is backed by the rigorous rules of judicial evidence: corroboration and documentation. SCM stories are not hearsay or gut-reaction testimonials. Rather, they are verifiable and confirmable accounts of the actions and results that real people have experienced using new tools and methods.

My colleagues and I have used the Success Case Method with many companies and agencies, large and small, over the past fifteen years. This includes a study about American Express Financial Advisors regarding the impact of their large and corporate-wide training program in emotional competence, an assessment of the effectiveness of the provision of laptop technology for sales representatives for a global furniture manufacturer, the introduction of new software by a Silicon Valley firm, and leadership training at the World Bank, to name just a few. We have conducted dozens of Success Case studies in pharmaceutical, computer, furniture, automobile dealership, rural development, child adoption, healthcare, welfare, retail, and manufacturing organizations, and even a Success Case study for the National Basketball Association (NBA).

The book is organized into eight chapters. Chapter One is an introduction to the Success Case Method (SCM), providing an overview of how it works, its rationale and basis in scientific inquiry, and the benefits it provides. The second chapter provides a more detailed step-by-step look at the SCM. Chapters Three through Seven are devoted to providing more how-to guidance and examples for each of the SCM steps, telling readers exactly how to proceed with their own SCM inquiries. For readers who do not have formal training or expertise in inquiry methods (though in most cases the application of the SC Method does not require these) a short list of resource readings in topics such as interviewing methods and inferential statistics is provided in the References section at the end of the book. Chapter Eight provides guidance for using the SCM in typical organizational settings and discusses the strategic applications for which SCM studies are especially useful. Finally, a complete (though sanitized) example of an actual Success Case study final report is referenced in Appendix A and can be found at both www.triadperform.com and www.bkconnection.com.

Throughout, the reader will find helpful illustrations, examples, checklists, and tools. The aim of the book is simple: I would like others to be able to use the Success Case Method as constructively and easily as

I have. Further, I hope that others will take this promising method to new levels of usefulness and development. The SCM has been revised considerably over the years. Although it works, and works well, like any other evolving human endeavor, it can surely be improved upon.

Acknowledgements

I am grateful for all those who, many years ago in my doctoral studies and early work, helped me learn about and build skills in program evaluation. These include Dale Brethower, Egon Guba, Jim Sanders, Geary Rummler, Michael Scriven, Dan Stufflebeam, and Ralph Tyler. I am especially indebted to my doctoral advisor, Malcolm Provus, who taught me how program evaluation could truly help people, programs, and knowledge grow. His untimely death cut short the brilliant life of a marvelous mentor and friend.

Thanks to Valerie Brown, Dennis Dressler, Tim Fallon, Shawn Merritt, and others at Triad Performance with whom I have planned and conducted dozens of Success Case evaluation studies. Without their help and earnest dedication, this model would not work as well as it does.

Lastly, I acknowledge our many and supportive clients who over the years have used the Success Case Method to help all of us learn and become more effective. Janet Costales and Sharon May at Compaq, Tamar Elkeles at QUALCOMM, Mary Brady at the World Bank, Scott Blanchard at Coaching.com, Bill Patrick and Jan Bocskay at the Family Independence Agency in Michigan, Karen Hudson-Samuels at Ford Motor Company, Sonya Fox at Corning, and Ara Yeramyan at Gap International are some of those who have pushed us hard and given enthusiastic support in return.

1

What is the Success Case Method and How Does it Work?

Truth, naked and cold, had been turned away from every door in the village. Her nakedness frightened the people. When Parable found her, she was huddled in a corner, shivering and hungry. Taking pity on her, Parable gathered her up and took her home. There, she dressed Truth in Story, warmed her, and sent her out again. Clothed in Story, Truth knocked again at the villagers' doors and was readily welcomed into the people's houses. They invited her to eat at their table and to warm herself by the fire.

Jewish Teaching Story (Simmons, 2001)

Organizations today are in a constant struggle to renew themselves and their processes, continuously trying out new ways of being more effective and competitive. People at all levels are faced with an endless parade of new technology, new ways of organization, new tools, new methods, new training programs, new jobs, and so on.

- An automobile manufacturer introduces a new team assembly approach
- A furniture company employs laptop computers to help salespeople present a dizzying array of potential office configurations
- Ambulance crews use wireless communications to communicate with a remote physician who provides real-time directions for care
- Airline security staff have access to new databases to scan passengers in an attempt to spot likely candidates for increased scrutiny
- Telecommunications operators receive listening training to help them better establish rapport, in an attempt to increase customer satisfaction
- A hotel chain provides cash incentives to housecleaning staff to help drive repeat business

How successful these innovations will be is anyone's guess, but what is always known is this: Some parts of these new initiatives will work some of the time with some of the people; other parts will work barely at all. Some people will experience success, and others will be frustrated and fail. Almost never will any of these changes work perfectly well with everyone. On the other hand, it is also unlikely that these changes will be a total failure—someone, somehow, will make at least some of them work.

Those whose job it is to make them work have a daunting challenge. They must have some ways of finding out—as quickly and easily as possible—which things are working and which are not; what parts of new innovations are working well enough to be left alone, which need revision, and which should be abandoned.

The Success Case Method (SCM) is designed to confront and leverage this reality. The partial success of a new initiative, no matter how small it is or how few are able to make it work is, nonetheless, success, and success is what we are aiming for. The SCM searches out and surfaces these successes, bringing them to light in persuasive and compelling stories so that they can be weighed (are they good enough?), provided as motivating and concrete examples to others, and learned from so that we have a better understanding of why things worked, and why they did not. With this knowledge, success can be built on and extended; faltering efforts can be changed or abandoned, and premising efforts can be noticed and nurtured.

But most change leaders and managers are in a bind. On the one hand, they have to guide and manage new innovations to make things work better, and on the other hand, they have very little time to find out what they need to know to do this. The easiest way to find out if things are working is to rely on hunches, guesses, and informal bits of information picked up here and there. These casual methods, however, leave too much room for error and misinformation. At the other end of the spectrum are full-blown audits, program reviews, and formal evaluation studies, but these are almost always too costly and time consuming and can end up providing too much information, too late to be helpful, or in such a dry and abstract form that no one pays attention.

In between is the SC Method, a relatively quick and easy method of finding out what is working and what is not, which also provides accurate and trustworthy information that can be used to make timely decisions.

Storytelling is at the heart of the SCM, and the principal output of an SCM study is stories. Across human history, stories are what we have used to understand and make sense of the world around us. We use stories because they have, for untold millennia, enchanted, moved, and entertained us. Stories tap deep emotion and command attention. All of us remember our favorite stories from childhood and will recall with fond emotion the warmth and comfort of a storytelling session.

Stories, however, can also be suspicious and questionable, as in fables and fantasies. We will probably remember as children that we were admonished not to "tell a story" (that is, a lie). The SCM deals with the suspicion that stories can generate in two key ways. First, we don't use the SCM to find and tell just any old story. We seek out and document the best, and the worst, that a new change or innovation is producing, and carefully capture the essence of these positive and negative experiences in carefully documented stories. The second way that the SCM produces credibility and persuasiveness is with truthfulness. SCM stories are not hearsay evidence or opinion. As will be seen later in the book, they must be confirmable experiences that can be backed up with corroboration and evidence. A story that cannot be confirmed is not a success story. Our criterion for the veracity of a success story is that it must tell how a person actually used something, and the actual results they got, in a way that would "stand up in court."

The SCM is a carefully balanced blend of the ancient art of storytelling with more modern methods and principles of rigorous evaluative inquiry and research. But the SCM is also practical. We employ sound principles of inquiry to seek out the right stories to tell, and we back them up with solid evidence. On the other hand, we don't try to tell all the stories that could be told, nor go overboard with exhaustive data collection and statistical analyses.

A Story of the Importance of Credibility in a Story

A recent experience in reporting the results of a corporate innovation will make the importance of this point clear. My colleagues and I had concluded an SCM study of the use of newly trained emotional intelligence skills in a financial planning company. One of the success stories we told was very dramatic— obviously so dramatic that some in our audience found it difficult to believe. One financial advisor, we had discovered, had used her emotional intelligence training to hugely increase her sales productivity. Before her training, she had ranked dead last in her region, managing less than $250,000 in assets, placing her in the bottom 10% of all advisors nationally. Eight months after the training, and after clearly and specifically using some of her training in making new appointments and closing sales, she was managing more than $1.6 million in assets and was ranked in the top 15% of advisors nationally. She had risen to the number two sales producer in her region.

We had been warned beforehand that some executives in our audience might be skeptical, even harshly so. Sure enough, one quite senior executive took a very dim view of the training and decided to confront us. I had just finished reporting the general success of the program (many advisors had similar, though less dramatic results) and had told the story of Anne, the advisor noted previously. Before we could present any of our corroborating evidence, this person in the audience interjected a loud guffaw. Immediately after this barking interruption, he stood and stated loudly for all to hear that: (a) the training was really a bunch of "malarkey" (my words, not his), (b) that this advisor probably exaggerated her results and made up her story to tell us what we wanted to hear, and that (c) stories like these were just that: a "bunch of bs."

I paused thoughtfully and acknowledged his concern, admitting indeed that there was a certain chance that this story could have been a fabrication. Anyone, I noted, could and should make a choice to either believe, or not believe, the story of Anne. But if you choose to not believe her story, then here is what you must at the same time believe is true in order to disbelieve Anne's story:

- *Anne was lying.*
- *Her manager was lying.*
- *Her peer advisors were lying.*
- *The regional office had falsified its training records.*
- *Anne had falsified her customers' files and had defrauded these same customers.*
- *The trainer was lying.*
- *The regional office had falsified its sales and productivity records.*
- *The national database the company maintained had been corrupted.*
- *And finally, everyone involved—Anne, her manager, her peers, her customers, and the training department—had conspired to create this story and falsify the records that documented it.*

So, I noted in closing, if you believe that these things happened, then by all means you should reject this story, and your claim that this training does not work is quite true.

The executive took his seat and was quiet and complacent during the rest of the report session. On the plane returning from the meeting, my colleagues and I noted how thankful we were that we took the time to follow our own SCM rules for gathering corroborating and documenting evidence!

The Basic SCM Questions

An SCM study can be used to get answers to any, or all, of four (4) basic questions:

- What is really happening?
- What results, if any, is the program helping to produce?

- What is the value of the results?
- How could the initiative be improved?

The SC inquiry directed to these questions can range from the very simple to the more complex. At the simplest end of the spectrum, an SC inquiry can be used just to discover and illustrate the ways in which a new innovation is being used or helping determine whether anything good is happening as the result of a new program or change. More complex, an SC study can indicate what proportions of people, in what organizational units, are using new tools and methods, and what success they are having. At the even more complex end of the spectrum, an SC study can provide estimates of return-on-investment and help make decisions about how much more value a program is realistically capable of making above and beyond its current level of impact.

Here, in more detail are four basic SC questions and some illustrations to demonstrate the range of inquiry that might be directed to each:

1. *What is really happening?* This basic SC question has a range of applications. At the most fundamental end of the complexity spectrum, a quick SC study could be used to simply illustrate the sorts of things that are happening, and not happening, in a new initiative. In a company that was trying to introduce a new team approach to selling, for example, we quickly discovered that only a few of the intended team applications were really being implemented. Almost all sales reps, for instance, were meeting each week to plan their sales calls in conjunction with one another's schedules. But almost none of them were making joint sales calls, and competition was still relatively rampant, as fears of sharing commissions overrode desires to cooperate. In another study of usage of new laptops in a sales firm, we found that all but a few

applications were being effectively used. Some of the unused applications turned out to be incompatible with some of the sales reps equipment; others were tried but deemed to be too complex or otherwise not helpful.

In a more complex study of usage of simulators for training computer repair technicians, we found that usage varied dramatically among geographic districts. In some districts, regional managers were providing incentives to attend simulator training and had created innovative scheduling schemes to allow their staff to participate. Overall, however, the expensive simulator facility was under-used or misused by nearly 40% of all technicians. This represented huge waste, and service management took quick steps to remedy the situation.

Some of the more specific questions that Success Case studies can be used to answer are:

- Who is using the new methods, and who is not?
- What parts of new innovations are getting used, and what parts are not?
- How widespread is usage?
- What groups or subgroups are making the least, or most, use of new techniques?
- When are methods being used, and with whom?

2. *What results, if any, is the program helping to produce?* Even very simple SC studies can quickly gather evidence about the most poignant and compelling results that a change initiative is producing, and they can provide rich illustrations of these "best case" outcomes. In a recent study of an innovative online supervisory support system, for example, we found that some supervisors had

used the new tools and methods to increase production. Others had used the tools to decrease staff turnover. A few had used the methods to keep minor complaints and misunderstandings from escalating into costly grievances and legal suits.

Of course, if there are no positive outcomes for the program, the SC Method will quickly discover this fact. One company, for example, had invested in a training program that was meant to assist managers in helping their employees create development plans. As it turned out, hardly any of the managers even tried out the new approach, and only a few of these had led to new development plans for employees. Of the employees who did create development plans, none felt that the process was constructive. Fortunately, this SC study was conducted after only a small pilot test of the program was implemented, so little damage was done and there was time to reconsider the entire initiative.

The SC study can be used to discover intended as well as unintended outcomes. In a similar study of another company trying out a new development planning approach, it was likewise discovered that only a few employees actually created formal development plans. But, it also became clear that the dialogue that the program stimulated between managers and employees was viewed as highly constructive. In almost every case, employees whose managers engaged them in a planning discussion felt more valued and understood. As it turned out, the managers of these appreciative employees used only a very small part of the intended process, but that single part turned out to be highly effective. As a result of this unintended outcome, the process was drastically simplified and distributed to many more managers.

It is very easy to combine estimates of results with estimates of how many people are making different sorts of use of a program. For example, in one SC study we concluded that "Sixty percent of the participants used the program to accomplish worthwhile results that are either helping to drive more new sales, retain customers, or increase revenues-per-customer. Of these successful participants, one out of five (20%) have achieved profit margins in excess of the company's goal of 15%. On the other hand, 28% of the program's participants have reported no use of the program's tools at all and are likewise achieving no impact on sales, retention, or revenue. The remaining 12% have reported some success, but their accomplishments are below profit margin expectations."

3. *What is the value of the results?* In many cases, and when it is desirable to do so, it is possible to extend the SC Method to estimate the dollar value of the successful results being achieved. In one case, a pharmaceutical sales rep used a new sales leadership technique to help secure a new HMO client worth annual sales revenues in excess of $5 million. In another instance, a production supervisor used some online support tools to defuse a sexual harassment problem and eventually avoid a costly lawsuit

When dollar values of results are estimated, they can then be compared to the costs of the program, and an ROI (return-on-investment) or cost-return comparison estimate can be made. In the case of the pharmaceutical sales rep who won the big account, it was evident that the profits on the increased revenues would have covered the costs for him and all his colleagues to participate in the sales effectiveness program.

Such value and cost estimates are, of course, only as good as the cost and value assumptions on which they are based. Such estimates are never complete, and assumptions are always open to question and debate. For these reasons, we usually avoid making value and cost-return claims except where such claims are clearly and uncontroversially defensible. In the case of the financial advisor who used a support program to increase her productivity, there was no arguing with her results; the record of accomplishment was valid and public. Further, there was incontrovertible evidence that she had used the new techniques with her clients and that this usage was brand new to her. Further, her manager agreed that she had mastered the new technique and used it regularly. Likewise, it was clear from training records that she had used the intended resources in the intended ways. Finally, both she and her manager were adamant that the success could not have been achieved had it not been for use of the new method. Given this, we felt comfortable that any reasonable person should have to accept our conclusion that the program had indeed produced a worthy result.

Sometimes, it is useful to combine estimates of the dollar-value of results with estimates of the scope and distribution of usage of new methods and tools. This sort of combination of Success Case data produces what we call an estimate of the "unrealized value" of the program. In other words, if a new initiative is shown to be producing good results, but for only a small portion of participants, then it is possible that there is a considerably larger amount of value yet to be gleaned from that program. In other words, the "good news" is that the program can work, and when it does, it produces valuable results. The "bad news" is that only a few participants are getting these results. But maybe this is really "good news," because if more people got the same results, then a lot more benefit would be realized.

In a recent study of a new supervisory database in a large company, for example, we were able to show that the program was probably "leaving more than a million dollars of value on the table." That is, the SC study provided clearcut and convincing evidence that the program was capable of producing highly valuable results. On the other hand, it was producing highly successful results with only a relatively small handful of participants. By making some modest changes in the program and helping managers of users be more supportive, a 20% increase in the number of successful users—at just half the level of effectiveness of the most successful users—could produce benefits worth several million dollars. It was quite clear from the SC data that a 20% increase in usage was not an unreasonable expectation.

4. *How could the initiative be improved?* This SC question extends the inquiry to assess those program factors that are associated with success, so that additional program users can increase their success and come closer to the very highest levels of success being achieved by the most successful users. Often, it is not the program's tools or methods themselves that are making the greatest difference in success, but certain workplace environmental factors are being leveraged to make the innovation work. In a training program, for example, it may be that one part of the organization uses an additional incentive and that this incentive combined with the training is achieving unparalleled results. This sort of SC inquiry helps to pinpoint the success-adding factors and enables suggestions to maximize the impact for all participants.

If it is found that an initiative is helping some people achieve valuable results, and it is also apparent that more results of the same (or better) value would be both possible and worthwhile, then it makes sense to identify ways to improve the initiative. In a study of a large computer company's use of a simulator facility, for example, we discovered that a large number of users had not ever used their simulator training in a client engagement. It was clear from comparing success with nonsuccess stories (a frequently used SC technique) that many technicians were being sent to the simulator training even though they had no current clients who had purchased the server equipment that the simulator training targeted. Managers of technicians were, apparently, combining flawed sales forecast data with their own misunderstanding of the nature and purpose of the simulator facility to send technicians to training when it was not needed. Senior leaders used the SC results to help service managers do a better job of scheduling their technicians for training. As a result, the usage of simulator training to achieve worthwhile client service outcomes improved from less than 60% to more than 90%. This outcome was of great benefit to the company because the simulator had previously been fully booked (with lots of people who didn't need it) and there was a waiting list for additional technicians to get access—some of whom really did need the training to meet customer needs. Interestingly, all of the positive changes to get more value from this training facility were made without revising anything at all about the training or simulator itself.

Uses for the Success Case Approach

The Success Case Method has a variety of beneficial uses. As the years have progressed and we have conducted more studies in a range of settings, new benefits have emerged, and I am convinced that readers who use the method will experience more yet. In Chapter Eight, several strategic SCM uses are discussed in more detail. Here, though, is a summary of the SC uses that are most common.

- *Quickly and easily discover what is working and what is not with new changes and initiatives.* Any new change initiative is highly predictable in one respect: It will almost never be entirely successful, nor will it likely be a total bust. Something good comes from almost anything new. With a new initiative that is getting mostly good results, the challenge is to sort the wheat from the chaff in that new initiative and leverage its successful components for greater impact. With an initiative that is mostly not working, the trick is to avoid throwing the baby out with the bathwater; those few elements of the program that are worth saving must be recognized and leveraged for a greater return.

- *Illustrate results and accomplishments in a way that is interesting and compelling.* Even when a program is doing well, there will always be some people who question its effectiveness and will want to see proof that it is making a difference. Because it uses stories of actual users getting real results of demonstrable value, the SC Method produces compelling and dramatic illustrations. The SC stories capture the attention of people and provide them with hard-to-argue-with evidence.

- *Identify best practices and increase the knowledge base of an organization.* A leader at the computer company Hewlett Packard is purported to have said, when asked what might make the company even more successful "If only Hewlett Packard knew what Hewlett Packard knows." Many knowledge management research studies have shown that companies rarely fully recognize and share the expertise within their own walls. Successful practices can go unrecognized for years, dramatically slowing the pace of competitive improvement. The SC Method can be used to quickly unearth best practices and diffuse them into the working knowledge base of the organization in a rapid and convincing way.

- *Provide models and examples to motivate and guide others.* In a similar vein, the SC Method helps new users of an innovation discover the ways in which others have applied tools and methods, serving as a guide and inspiration for their own practice. A common reaction among trainees who return from a training session is this: "I really enjoyed it and I learned some good stuff. But I'm really not sure exactly how I could use it in my job." The SC Method is especially helpful in overcoming this problem because it provides new trainees (or others struggling to adopt an innovation) with a concrete and specific illustration of exactly how some of their peers have put something to use and made it work.

- *Meet demands, quickly and practically, to evaluate the success or failure of a new initiative.* At some point, a new program or change comes under critical scrutiny and review. The SC Method is a powerful and convincing evaluation approach that provides compelling evidence—evidence that would "stand up in court"—about how well a program is working and what sort of valuable results (if any) it is producing.

How the Success Case Method Works

An SC study has a very simple, two-part structure. The first part of an SC study entails locating potential and likely "success cases"—those individuals (or teams) that have apparently been the most successful in using some new change or method. This first step is often accomplished with a survey. Although a survey is often used, it is not always necessary. It may be possible to identify potential success cases by reviewing usage records and reports, accessing performance data, or simply by asking people—tapping into the "information grapevine" of the organization. A survey is most often used, however, because it provides the additional advantage of extrapolating results to get quantitative estimates of the proportions of people who report using, or not using, some new method or innovation. Also, when careful sampling methods are employed, then probability estimates of the nature and scope of success can also be determined.

In the second part of an SC study, we interview the handful of identified success cases to determine and document the actual nature of success being achieved. The first portion of the interview is aimed at "screening." In this part, we try to quickly determine whether the person being interviewed represents a true and verifiable success. Assuming that this is true, the interview then proceeds to probe, understand, and document the success. This interview portion of the study provides us with "stories" of use and results. Importantly, these interviews focus on the gathering of verifiable and documentable evidence so that success can be "proven." Typically, an SC study results in only a small number of documented success cases—just enough to poignantly illustrate the nature and scope of the success the program is helping to produce. In our study of success with emotional intelligence training, for example, we surveyed several hundred financial advisors. In the end, however, it was necessary to report only five success case stories in order to amply and fairly illustrate the impact of the program.

Almost always, an SC study also looks at instances of nonsuccess. That is, just as there is some small extreme group who has been very successful in using a new approach or tool, there is a likewise some small extreme group at the other end who experienced no use or value. Investigation into the reasons for lack of success can be very enlightening and useful. Comparisons between the groups are especially useful. In the case of successful use of laptops by sales reps, for example, we found that almost every successful user reported that his or her district manager provided training and support in the use of the new laptop. Conversely, a lack of district manager support was noticed in almost every instance of lack of success. Identifying and reporting the apparent factors that made the difference between success and lack of it (notice we avoid the use of the word failure) can be a great help in making decisions to improve a program's impact.

Foundations of the Success Case Method

As already noted, the Success Case Method combines the ancient craft of storytelling with the more current evaluation approaches of naturalistic inquiry and case study. It often (though not always) employs simple survey and questionnaire methods. It also employs the social inquiry process of key informants, which is a sociologist's fancy term for the notion that, when you want to know something, you should talk to the people who know the most about it. The SCM borrows a bit of methodology from journalism and judicial inquiry. In a way, we are journalists looking for a few dramatic and "newsworthy" stories of success and nonsuccess. When we find them, we seek corroborating evidence and documentation to be sure that the success story is defensible and thus reportable.

The Success Case Method likewise leverages the measurement approach of analyzing extreme groups, because these extremes are masked when mean and other central tendency measures are employed. This is the same concept applied in Shainan quality methods that are employed in some manufacturing operations to assess and diagnose quality of machine parts. The Shainan method directs quality assessors to analyze a sample of the very best parts produced by a manufacturing process as well as a sample of the very worst. From these extreme samples, manufacturing process elements are targeted and revised to assure a greater consistency of only "BOB" (the best of the best) parts and reduce the frequency of "WOW" (worst of the worst) parts.

Stories are also at the heart of the SC approach. Storytelling is as old as people themselves and has always been a powerful influencer. Although there has been some psychological research on the power of stories and storytelling, it is probably not necessary to review it, because the power of stories is well known to most of us from our life experience in general. My first encounter as an evaluation practitioner with the power of stories was highly instructive.

Meet Sonia Morningstar

I was a graduate student providing technical support to the U.S. Office of Education (USOE) during budget hearings in front of congressional oversight committees. One USOE program officer, making a plea for funds, had just delivered a lengthy presentation, with many mind-numbing graphs, charts, and statistics that were intended to show the breadth and characteristics of the many audiences served in his program area. The yawns of the bored and inattentive congressional representatives were almost audible. The presenter was thanked for his pallid presentation and advised that decisions would be pending.

Then a second program officer came to the podium. He held up a large photograph of an obviously poor, young Native American child, dressed in dirty and tattered clothing, clutching a worn schoolbook in her dirt-covered hands. "Meet Sonia Morningstar," he intoned. The panel representatives were immediately attentive. The presenter went on to briefly tell the story of little Sonia, who had been born years earlier in a dirt-floored hogan in the arid Southwest near the Mexican border. His tale retold how she had attended a local school where she was fortunate enough (thanks to the astute funding decisions of this very panel) to have been provided with special attention to her learning deficits. To the greater surprise of the audience, Sonia herself—now five years older and dressed in neat and simple native garb, materialized next to the program officer. She thanked the panel for their efforts on her behalf and spoke humbly about her success in mastering reading skills. She was now, she told them, the first person in her family to succeed in high school, was working in a medical clinic after school, and had already secured a foundation scholarship for medical school.

●━━━━━━━━━━━━━━━━━━━━━━━━━━━━━━●

The congressional panel members applauded at the end of her talk, and, one at a time, stood to shake her hand. They thanked the program officer and asked a few questions about how many others like Sonia were being helped by their funding (for which the program officer had ready responses and even a concise chart). As clearly as they could promise within the constraints of their agenda, they assured the program officer that continued funding would be forthcoming. This happened more than thirty-two years ago. Yet I remember clearly to this day the bright, beaded necklace on the child's throat, the glisten of the tear I saw in the eye of one of the panel members, and the lump in my own throat as I listened to her compelling tale.

As already noted, a Success Case study begins with a search for stories of success worthy of the telling. Once these apparent success cases are identified, we then interview them (using a method to be explained in more detail later in the book). If the qualification phase of the interview uncovers evidence of results that could be verified, the interview proceeds to document the nature and scope of the success. It also seeks to determine why that person was successful—especially to identify the organizational factors, supervisory assistance, for example, that supported and enabled the success. Again, a success case is not a testimonial of emotional reactions or other favorable feelings. Rather, it is a detailed and objective story about action and behavior, relating exactly how something was used, what results were achieved, and what specific factors enabled or interfered with success. Even more important, a success story must be confirmable and supported with verifiable evidence. A success story is not considered valid and reportable until we are convinced that we have enough compelling evidence that the story would "stand up in court"—that indeed, the case the story relates is a true success, and we could, if pressed, prove it beyond a reasonable doubt.

Other evaluators and researchers have used approaches similar to the Success Case Method. Bob Stake at the University of Illinois has long promoted the use of illustrative case studies (Stake, 1995). Egon Guba (Guba & Lincoln, 1985) and others have promoted the use of naturalistic inquiry and case methods. These are just a few of the practitioners and theoreticians whose thinking has influenced the creation of the SCM. As sometimes happens, inventors follow parallel paths of discovery unbeknownst to one another. Barry Kibel, author of the book *Success Stories as Hard Data* (Kibel, 1999) is a case in point (after finding his book, I was interested to note that we had very similar academic training and were influenced by the same evaluation progenitors). Kibel's work is used in social welfare settings and employs success stories, but applies a considerably complex and rigorous quantitative scoring method to the stories to compare program outcomes.

Here is an interesting story of an SC study that some colleagues and I conducted recently. It illustrates nicely some of the ways that the SCM is rooted in solid scientific and evaluative inquiry. It also shows how the SCM can be used to fruitfully respond to and cope with some tricky organizational scenarios.

A Success Case Beer Story

Human resources executives in a multimillion-dollar national beer distributor named "Bulltoad" asked my colleagues and I to help them solve a vexing and important business problem they had encountered in attempting to implement a change in operations. First, a little background: This beer distributorship was one of several hundred such firms, all exclusively licensed by the national brewery to sell beer to retail outlets (supermarkets, convenience stores, and so forth) in specific geographical regions. The national brewery demanded that each distributorship adhere to certain quality standards and procedures. In this case, the national distributor had initiated a "freshness date stamp" campaign, which was intended to assure consumers of the freshness of the product. As part of this campaign, all distributors were required to keep the cases of beer refrigerated at all times. The human resources executives were having a bit of a problem working with one of the key distributorships.

Prior to the change, beer truck drivers (who were also the sales force) drove their fully loaded trucks to each potential retail buyer, tried to sell what they could, then returned at the end of the day. On their return, the truck would be parked in a locked and guarded lot. The next morning, warehouse loaders would get more beer from the cooler and replenish the truckload, which was then driven out on a new route. Under the new freshness campaign requirements, the unsold beer had to be unloaded and put back into refrigerated coolers, then totally reloaded the next morning. The distributor owner (a feisty and voluble eighty-six-year-old woman) was considerably concerned and somewhat angry about this new change, as it could drastically increase her costs. Not only would the electric bill for refrigeration go up, but also the increased handling would create damaged cases, which could then not be resold to retailers. No, she said, this whole freshness campaign was a sorry affair and would drive her to an earlier grave, if not out of business.

Unfortunately, she was very nearly right. The average route sales driver returned with nearly 40% of the load unsold, thus dramatically increasing the total amount of handling and refrigeration needed. Worse news yet, more than 80% of the sales route drivers returned with at least 30% of their beer load still on the truck. More warehouse loaders would need to be hired, and increased damage was virtually assured. But there was a small ray of hope. Our review of truck loading records showed that a small number of the drivers (just three of the total of fifty-two employed) returned consistently with a nearly empty truck. Further, since the announcement of the change in handling requirements just a month earlier, these three drivers had even improved their percentage of load sold. The improvement was slight, however, as they were already selling their trucks nearly empty each day since well before the new campaign began.

So, we had our handful of possible "success cases" identified. We then proceeded to interview each of them and dig into the how and why of their effective behavior. Though each of them was somewhat different, they approached their work in a very similar fashion. The story of their success was quite simple. First, each of them had worked closely with warehouse employees and had formed a sort of "partnership." They talked to the warehouse loaders frequently, told them what was working and what was not, and provided them with support and encouragement for the things they did right to help them. Secondly, these three salespeople took extra pains to understand the markets in which their key retail buyers operated. Each of them read the local newspapers, for example, and identified upcoming events (a college homecoming, a large family reunion, a softball tournament, for instance), which were traditional beer-consumption activities. Armed with this information, they guided their retail buyers' purchase decisions, encouraging large purchases when needed and suggesting cutbacks if market conditions seemed to indicate such a move. Interviews with some of these retail buyers confirmed this behavior and showed as well that the beer route driver was seen as a sort of "partner" by the retailer, a person who cared and could be trusted.

Clearly, there were a small number of clearly specific things these three drivers did that helped them adjust their loads on a daily basis, so that predicted sales and actual sales were highly congruent. They helped their warehouse loaders understand these requirements and left each day with a "customized" load of beer that was almost always totally sold.

A quick interview with a few of the drivers who did not sell all of their loads showed a very common though opposed approach. These drivers communicated only a little with the loaders and instead met in a local restaurant while the loaders were at work. As far as the loaders knew, the drivers expected a fully loaded truck. As one driver put it, "Don't ever let me down, friend. The last thing I need is a buyer who wants sixty cases, but I only got fifty on the truck!" With this sort of admonition in mind, the undirected warehouse loaders fully stocked each truck, each day. Of course, they complained bitterly about having to unload the unsold product each afternoon, but received little sympathy from the drivers. "My job ain't so easy either, pal. Get another job if you don't like this one."

Our analysis of the success cases allowed us to prescribe some specific new tasks and actions for all of the drivers to begin to use and some relatively simple training that the distributor owner could begin. We captured the stories from the few loaders, drivers, and retail customers on audiotape, which the owner found highly persuasive. Armed with this clear evidence and compelling direction, the owner embarked on a training intervention to teach all of the drivers and loaders the techniques that the few were using so successfully. The training alone was not sufficient, of course, but combined with a new (though remarkably small) pay incentive for matching actual sold loads to predicted loads, and some special coaching for drivers who had difficulty, the problem was eased in a short while. Within two months, the returned load percentage was at historical lows and improving weekly. The feared cost and damage increases never materialized, and our feisty owner went on to find new things to worry about.

Limitations of the Success Case Approach

As noted earlier, the SC Method is not a comprehensive and "one fix" sort of approach. Rather, it is a single but useful tool that change leaders and others can use to help them get the information they need to more effectively guide change initiatives. There are other evaluation approaches that are more comprehensive and thorough. But, of course, these are often more expensive and time-consuming.

The very simplicity of the SC Method causes some to raise important questions about its usefulness and validity. Here are some of the common questions, and an answer for each:

Question: *Isn't the SC Method biased because it looks only at a few cases?*

Answer: Yes. It is biased. An SC study intentionally looks for the most successful (and often the least successful) participants and outcomes. The SC approach rests on the assumption that it is very helpful to learn from those few users of a new innovation—the "pioneers"— who are experiencing the greatest success. Their experience can tell us a lot about how to make improvements and get even more success with more people. But, although the method is biased in its selection of cases to illustrate, the success stories themselves are very objective and rigorously supported with confirmable evidence.

Question: *How can you judge the whole success of a program based on just a few cases?*

Answer: You can't, and the SC Method does not try to. What we learn is this: If a program is working at all, then what is the best that it is doing? What seems to be working, and what is not? If the best that is being accomplished is not very good, or if hardly anyone is using anything, then we certainly have discovered something useful. But we shouldn't make an overall summative judgment without more evidence.

Question: *What about the "average" participant and the overall effect of a program?*

Answer: The SC approach is not concerned with the "average" as in typical, or statistical, mean performance. It is almost always true that a new initiative will work quite well with some people and not at all with others. When you add all these instances together and divide by the total number (as a quantitative analysis model requires you to do), then you can misrepresent the reality of the program. In fact, there may be no such thing as the "mean" participant, because all the action is at the extreme successful and nonsuccessful ends of the spectrum. Again, the SC Method looks for the very best that a program is accomplishing, because it is based on the assumption that this is well worth knowing.

Question: *Is the Success Case Method scientific?*

Answer: Yes, it is based on solid rules and the discipline of scientific inquiry. Success cases must be supported by verifiable and pertinent evidence. The interview portion of the SC Method relies on the rules of good naturalistic (e.g., case study) inquiry and reporting. Success Case stories should be thought of as judicial court testimony; they must be supported with evidence that would "stand up in court." The survey portion of an SC study follows the rules of good survey methods. When these rules are followed and solid sampling methods are employed, then it is entirely possible to make good-faith estimates about the breadth and scope of impact. That is, we might confidently create a conclusion such as "It is likely that 80% of all participants are achieving results of at least the same value."

Question: *Do you have to be an evaluation expert to use the Success Case Method?*

Answer: No. People with a reasonable amount of interpersonal skill and common sense can implement many simple SC studies. But it would sometimes be a good idea to get some expert assistance. When survey data will be relied on to make estimates of a broader scope of impact, it is recommended to use a person who has survey design and construction skills. Many organizations have people on staff with technical research skills who could, after reading this book, plan and implement a thorough and effective SC study. People who want to make use of the SC approach but who have no research or evaluation experience would be wise to get some expert help, using this book as a guide and resource.

Question: *How is the SCM different from other evaluation approaches?*

Answer: It is similar in that it uses many of the same tools of typical evaluation, such as survey, statistical analysis (sometimes), and interviewing. It is different, however, in that the SCM does not seek to be nor claim to be a comprehensive approach. Nor does the SCM try to make a summative judgment about the worth or merit of a change initiative. It just collects some information about it so that those responsible can figure out what parts of it seem to be working, what parts are not, and how they might make it more successful. If an SCM study found very little usage or impact, it could certainly lead to a more comprehensive study to decide whether to keep a program at all. Overall, the SCM is quite a bit more simple, faster, and often more credible than other more comprehensive evaluation methods. It is not intended to replace more rigorous and comprehensive evaluation, just offer an alternative and useful tool.

The next chapter provides a detailed look, step by step, at how to plan and conduct an SC study, be it very simple or more complex. This chapter also expands on the purposes for SC studies and provides a number of illuminating examples and illustrations.

2.

The Success Case Method: Step by Step

Designing and implementing an SC study may be quite simple or relatively complex, depending on the overall scope and purpose of the initiative. We have conducted SC studies, for instance, that were planned, designed, implemented, and completed in a period of about three weeks, consuming fewer than thirty or so hours of our time in total. We have also conducted SC studies that spanned half a year from start to finish and involved several hundred hours from a number of staff.

At the smaller end of the scale, we followed up just seven pharmaceutical sales representatives who were trying out some new methods and tools for soliciting business with health maintenance organizations (HMOs). Only one rep had had an opportunity to use the new tools, yet had experienced an especially successful sales call that leveraged the program's capability. This one successful instance was exactly the sort of application that the program sponsors had hoped for and served as an exemplary model for others to follow. In this case, the entire study was completed over a period of nine days, with only a few brief telephone calls.

At the other extreme, one of our SC projects looked at the impact of management development for an international child adoption and community development agency. This multimillion-dollar project employed trained field office managers from dozens of countries around the globe, most in very remote and rural areas, as this is where the principal work of the agency took place. Because impact was hypothesized to involve organizational change and work relationships among a number of office staff, field visits were deemed necessary to develop success profiles. Success Case interviews were conducted in person at several agency office locations. Given the remoteness of sites, our staff had to travel for several days (in one case by donkey when a rural bus broke down) just to get into the office locations.

Regardless of their complexity and scope, all Success Case studies follow the same major steps. In some cases, a study step may be completed very simply in a matter of minutes, in other cases this same step may involve several people and consume many days of effort over an extended period. In all cases, though, each step must be considered, planned for, designed, and implemented. This chapter provides a description of each step in the SCM process. Following chapters explain these steps in more detail, providing in-depth guidance and illustration.

The SCM Steps

There are five overall steps to be followed in planning and conducting an SC study.

1. Focusing and planning a Success Case study
2. Creating an "impact model" that defines what success should look like
3. Designing and implementing a survey to search for best and worst cases
4. Interviewing and documenting success cases
5. Communicating findings, conclusions, and recommendations

Depending on the purpose and scope of the study, some of the steps may have different subparts. Sometimes, for example, one purpose of the study is to determine how broadly an innovation has been adopted. In these instances, Step 3 (designing and implementing a survey to search for best and worst cases) will include a procedure for tapping different samples of job roles to assess how widespread certain application behaviors are being implemented among key innovation roles and audiences. Or, in a large SCM study, a complex reporting process may be required that provides different reports and presentations to different audiences.

1. Focusing and Planning a Success Case Study

This first step is focused on thinking through what will be required to conduct an effective study that will provide the information people need and expect. The principal aim of this step is first to clarify and understand what the study needs to accomplish, then be sure that all the necessary pieces of the study are indeed planned for so that the promise of the study will, in fact, be delivered.

Some of the key considerations and decisions that must be made as part of this first step are:

- *What is the purpose of the study?* An SC study may have one or more of a range of possible purposes. Depending on the purpose, or purposes, the design for the study will need to be . . . Some common purposes are:

  - To allay—or confirm—the fears of skeptics who question the results and worthiness of a new program
  - To determine what about a new program is working well enough to be maintained and what is not working that may require revision or deletion
  - To strengthen "marketing" of a program or initiatives by documenting real and noteworthy instances of success
  - To help managers in one part of an organization determine what they need to do to get their employees to achieve the greater success that managers in other parts of the organization are experiencing
  - To provide exemplary models of especially successful behavior and program applications that can be used to inspire and motivate others
  - To assess the return on investment of an initiative
  - To identify recommendations for revisions to improve impact
  - To help decide whether a pilot initiative is having a positive enough impact to justify a broader roll-out
  - To "de-bug" a hastily implemented solution

- *Who (what groups and individuals) want or need the study to be done, and why is it important to them?* There are typically several stakeholders in a program, and often these different stakeholders may have different needs and expectations or each might define success differently. It is always wise to be sure that these stakeholders are identified, that none are left out, and that their needs and expectations are fully understood.

- *What specific program or initiative is the study to be focused on?* If the impact of something is going to be assessed, it is critical to be explicit and precise about just what "it" is that is being assessed. Eventually, the study will draw inferences about how well that "something" worked or did not. What exactly is that "something"? It is vital to carefully define the program or initiative and to check that definition with all of the stakeholders to make sure that there is clear agreement.

- *What participants are involved in the program and how many or what portion of them should be included in the study?* Sometimes a study will investigate the success of an entire program. In many cases, however, it is more realistic or practical to look at just a subpart of the program. In a study of a nationwide technology innovation, for example, we focused only on just how well the program worked in branch offices, because this was where services were actually provided to customers. Or, the study might focus on certain categories of employees (managers, for example) even though a training program was provided to all employees of a company. Sometimes, this decision may entail the construction of a scientifically determined sample, such as a random or stratified sample.

- *What is the time frame for the study?* It is important to be clear and certain about when the results of the study are needed and when a report would be most useful. If a study is needed to inform a decision about whether a pilot program is ready for broader roll-out, then it is necessary to know when the roll-out decision is to be made, to be sure the study will be completed by that date.

- *What resources are available for completing the study?* There are many levels of detail and complexity that are possible for a Success Case study. The final plan for the study is always a "best fit" between what is needed to fulfill the purpose for the study and what is available to spend on the study. Often, changes must be made to reduce the scope of the study in some ways in order to reduce costs or to increase the resources available to enable the purpose to be fulfilled.

- *What overall strategy for the study will work best?* This final portion of the first step pulls together all of the information gleaned about purposes, stakeholders, resources available, and so forth. The idea is to arrive at a study strategy that will work most effectively and efficiently to fulfill the purpose of the study in the time frame needed. The Success Case Method is a general approach to assessment and evaluation. Any particular SCM study, however, is a unique application of the more general method. One study we did, for example, used a survey to identify potential success cases, then included in-person, on-site interviews. In another study, we identified potential success cases "through the grapevine" to acquire recommendations and potential leads on successes, then used telephone interviews to determine the best cases for final documentation. In yet another study done for a major automobile manufacturer, success cases were defined as particular automobile dealerships versus individual people, and we investigated impact at the level of the entire dealership. Each SCM study is unique, tailored to meet the special needs, requirements, and constraints of the particular situation.

Chapter Three provides more detailed guidance in completion of this first step in the SCM process.

2. Creating an Impact Model that Defines What Success Should Look Like

The "impact model" is a projection of what success would look like if the initiative (the technology change, the training, for example) were really working. That is, the impact model portrays what successful behaviors and results should be found if the program were working well. This portrayal of success is then used to guide the actual inquiry.

Consider, for instance, an example in which sales representatives were supposed to be using new laptop technology to achieve greater sales volume. In this case, our discussions with stakeholders determined that sales reps were, ideally, to use the laptops in five key ways:

1. To analyze market segments to identify the high leverage accounts
2. To analyze accounts to prepare a client account profile and identify high-leverage sales opportunities
3. To prepare a customized sales presentation keyed to the client profile
4. To present persuasive information to the client
5. To track sales performance and continuously update their market database.

For these applications, we then identified one or more outcomes (impact results) that the laptop applications, if they were successful, would achieve. This model of intended uses and outcomes would then used (in the next SCM step) to create a survey to identify those sales reps that were actually using their laptops for any of these applications. In addition, the impact model would also be used to guide our interviews of possible success cases, which of course then illustrated the actual impact of the innovation.

Table 2.1 provides an example of the impact model created for such a sales representative laptop initiative.

In some cases, the impact model definition is very simple. Consider, for instance, the example from Chapter One of the beer sales and delivery problems. In this case, because we didn't know what successful people might actually be doing, the impact model was simply an outcome: The return of the delivery truck with little or no unsold beer. This single outcome was used to identify specific drivers, then the interviews with these drivers revealed the behaviors and actions that helped achieve these outcomes. In other cases, the intended uses of a technology or intervention might be clearly defined, though the outcome or impact is not known. In these cases, a more behavioral impact model is created, which is then used (usually through a written survey) to identify potential success cases, as in the laptop example.

In any case, whether it is simple or more complex, it is critical to "picture" success—create a projected image of what success should appear like if it is being realized. This projected image then helps focus and drive the inquiry to locate and understand actual success. The impact model is also useful in helping resolve and clarify any misunderstandings of the program to be studied as it was first defined in Step 1. Chapter Four contains several examples of impact models for different SCM study scenarios and provides more detailed guidance on how to construct a useful impact model.

3. Designing and Implementing a Survey to Search for Best and Worst Cases

Sometimes the location and identification of success cases is very simple and does not require a written survey. In one study of the use of some new leadership training, our "survey" consisted simply of asking a few senior executives to tell us which of their branch managers were

Table 2.1 Impact Model for Pharmaceutical Sales Representative Laptop Initiative

Capabilities	Critical Applications	Key Results	Business Goals
Sales reps with:			
Understanding of laptop potential	Analyze market segments to identify the high leverage accounts	Higher percentage of sales efforts dedicated to high-leverage strategic accounts	Increased market share for key products
Ability to operate laptop hardware	Analyze accounts to prepare a client account profile and identify high-leverage sales opportunities	Sales presentations customized to address account-specific opportunities	Increased profits
Ability to use laptop software	Prepare a customized sales presentation keyed to the client profile	Increased sales to key accounts	
Access to company intranet	present persuasive information to the client–	Increased market share for high-leverage products in key accounts	
	track sales performance and continuously update their market database		

doing the best job is using these new skills. Those names that were referred to us by the most executives were then the branch managers who we called to inquire further.

When just a simple identification of possible success cases is needed, there are several survey methods that do not require a formal and written questionnaire that is sent to program participants. These range from as simple a method as just asking, as in the laptop example, to analyzing performance records or other data. Consider, for example, an SCM study of automobile mechanics and how well they were using (or not using) a new online computer diagnostic tool provided in the repair bays of automobile dealers. In this study, a search of repair records could identify those mechanics who had the best and the worst repair records (fastest repair time, no need for rework, no complaint, etc.). We could then interview a sample of each of these to determine which group—the best or the worst—used or did not use the computer tools. Thus, the survey was simply an analysis of existing records to identify success cases.

But most often, a Success Case study uses a brief written survey that is sent to program participants. The written survey usually provides more information about where in the organization success is being most, and least, experienced. And, the written survey enables an analysis of the proportions of different types of participants that are experiencing the greatest and least amounts of success.

The Success Case survey is typically sent by email, because this is the fastest and simplest way for respondents to reply. This written survey simply lists the key behaviors, tasks, actions, tools, and so forth that we think are most associated with success (derived from the impact model created in the previous step). The survey then asks respondents to report which of these key actions and tools they are using, and which results, if any, they are achieving. When surveys are returned, we create a "scoring" scheme to help us sort responses from the very highest to the very lowest so that we can decide who is a "success" and who is not. Then we analyze the response data to identify possible success cases— both the best and the worst. These people are interviewed to describe and document their success experiences.

The length and complexity of the survey process depends on what information is needed, which is in turn driven by the purpose for the study. If the purpose includes trying to identify the several factors and characteristics that are associated with success and/or the breadth of success, or where in the organization the most success is being achieved, then the survey will have to be more complex. The survey might, for example, need to be partitioned into subsurveys to assess success for different job roles. In a recent study for the State of Michigan, for example, we needed to gauge the success of a major training initiative for child welfare workers. In this case, we had to first identify those job roles (office directors, for example) that were most important to survey, structure stratified samples for each job role, then create a different form of the survey for each of these different roles. This survey had a two-fold purpose. First, it was used to identify potential success cases for each of the several roles. Secondly, because we sent the survey to carefully defined samples of people in each role, it allowed us to esti- mate how widespread the impact of the training was across the state for each of the several roles.

Analysis conducted in Step 1—focusing—helps determine how complex this fourth step needs to be as well as what sort of survey process (written, survey of records, asking for referrals, etc.) will be needed. Chapter Five provides guidance and illustrations of the com- pletion of the survey step.

4.   Interviewing and Documenting Success Cases

This step is typically the most time consuming but also produces the most and the richest information of the study. The interview process is both open ended and highly structured. It is open ended in that we have to be open and ready to discover information that we did not expect and to doggedly follow leads and "hunches." The aim is to capture and document the very particular and personal ways in which an innovation or intervention has been used to achieve successful results. Thus, we have to let the Success Case interviewees lead us, tell their stories freely, and be open to learn from them. If, after all, we knew exactly what their success was, and thus could predict every response and nuance, there would be no need for this method in the first place.

At the same time, a high degree of structure is needed to be sure that all of the critical dimensions of success are covered and that the success story is credible and accurate. We also need to search for and identify those performance environment factors (supervisory support, incentives, tools, and so forth) that have enabled these most successful people to be successful. This requires discipline and an adherence to a structured inquiry method on the part of the interviewer. For reasons of practicality, a Success Case interview usually cannot last for longer than forty-five minutes to an hour, so there is a lot of information to be gleaned in a relatively short while. So, although the interviewer is open to new information and discoveries, there are nonetheless particular bases to be covered, thus he or she must firmly guide the interview and ask sharply targeted questions.

The Success Case interview has two major parts. In the first part, we "qualify" the success case. That is, we ask questions to be sure that this person (or team) has, indeed, utilized something from the intervention or innovation under study to achieve some worthwhile result. Sometimes, a person's survey will indicate that the respondent has achieved a success. But, on probing, we find that the person really has not achieved success or that there is simply no evidence (other than their own perceptions) to support their claim. Because the Success Case study needs to not only document and explain success, but to "prove" it, the unverifiable success case has to be left out.

The second portion of the interview, assuming that there is really a success to document, goes on to probe and flesh out the story of success. This not only explains and illustrates the success but also seeks to identify the factors that made success possible.

Finally, the interview step of the success study concludes with a write-up of success cases. This is done following a prescribed format, several examples of which are included in Chapter Six. Chapter Six also covers the interview process in detail, and it includes an overall interview structure as well as several examples of probing questions and interview guides.

5. Communicating Findings, Conclusions, and Recommendations

The final step in a Success Case study is the communication of the results to several interested stakeholders. Because we hope that a Success Case study will lead to action, such as decisions to make an intervention more successful, the communication step usually includes some sort of process to help stakeholders understand the results and reach consensus on the study's implications. In fact, we intentionally dislike and avoid calling this final step a "report," as often reports are just one-way transmissions of information that receive insufficient attention and do not lead to action. Assuming that the Success Case study has indeed surfaced some useful and actionable information, then we want to be sure that our stakeholders pay maximum attention to it. Thus, we almost always recommend that a meeting be convened to discuss the results of the study. Then, we facilitate this meeting so that certain implications are raised and confronted, and we try to lead the group of stakeholders to arrive at an agreement to take action—assuming, of course, that some such action is warranted by the findings.

Chapter Seven includes an outline for a Success Case study report, highlighting the major categories of findings, conclusions, and recommendations. This chapter also includes illustrations and examples of actual Success Case reports as well as example agendas for stakeholder meetings to review the findings.

Where the Steps Came From— The Accidental SCM Study

I have chosen to close this chapter with a story of my own about an evaluation I conducted before I had created and named the Success Case Method. This incident was the point at which I turned in frustration away from the more traditional evaluation methods I had been using and began to create the steps and procedures of the Success Case approach.

The client was a large pharmaceutical corporation that developed and marketed prescription drugs. Driven by shifting market demands and the need for more profitable sales, the company had initiated a new sales process wherein field sales representatives would employ a more targeted selling approach. The new sales method was quite complex and required sales reps to analyze major current and potential accounts using a number of sophisticated tools and methods. As part of the shift to the new sales strategy, sales reps had been involved in a training program to learn the new tools and methods.

The evaluation questions the client had were quite simple: Is the training good enough to change actual selling behavior in the field, and what if anything should we do to improve it? The rationale for the evaluation was equally simple. The sales strategy was part of a larger strategy to improve profits and market penetration for key products and was seen as critical to competitive advantage. If sales actions and results didn't change, then the overall strategy would not succeed. The training was therefore important. It had to work. It was also early in the deployment of the training program, thus the client needed to know what, if anything, should be done to improve the training and be sure it worked as well as it needed to.

My charge was simple: I was to assess the impact of the training, and make recommendations to the client as to how it could be improved.

I started by reviewing records from the training program that was conducted as a part of the initiative. To my surprise, I learned that there was a considerable database from the training program and that there was already evidence that the training was quite effective, at least in an immediate sense. The training department had created and administered a performance test at the conclusion of the program to assess whether sales reps had really mastered the new analysis techniques and how to use the various planning tools. My review of the test itself showed that it was an excellent measuring process (it had been developed in conjunction with a local university using graduate students from a highly regarded human performance technology program). Not only was the test excellent, but it was clear from the scores of trainee sales reps that the training worked very well—at the conclusion of training, at least all of the sales reps had achieved mastery scores in excess of 85%.

Given the fact that, at the end of the training, all of the sales reps were fully capable of using the new, targeted selling tools and methods, it was clear that the client's question really focused on the transfer of the training. That is, the issue was whether the new methods and tools were being used effectively on the job after the training was completed.

Time was very short in this evaluation. The client needed results quickly. There was no time for a survey of all, or even a lot of, the participants. I decided, then, to just begin by interviewing some of the program's participants, figuring that I could learn enough from talking to a few of them to find out what about the training was working in the field and what was not. I further decided to start my interviews with those few sales reps for whom the training had been most initially successful—those who had best mastered skills in the new methods and tools according to the end-of-program test results. If these few were not able to use the new techniques in the field, I thought, then I could be sure the training was not sufficient. Further, those who had learned the most were most likely to have tried the most of the new methods and tools, so the client could figure out what parts of the training were, or were not, working in actual field applications. I chose interviewees according to the following criteria:

- *They were working in key markets with customers who were in a position to purchase the most profitable products and were thus in roles where use of the new methods was not only most crucial, but most likely.*
- *They had reported (on a post-training reaction questionnaire) that the training was excellent and that they were anxious to begin to use it to not only raise sales but to increase their chances for higher commissions.*
- *They had scored the highest on the mastery test administered at the completion of the training. In other words when they left the training, they knew how to do it better than anyone else did. If this amount of skill proved to be insufficient, then the training would need revision.*

It was quite easy, referring to the mastery test, to understand exactly how a sales rep was supposed to use the training in the field. Though I had not created the notion of an "impact model" yet, I had a sense for the specific behaviors, tools, and sales outcomes that one would expect a sales rep should demonstrate if he or she was using the methods correctly.

Of the fifty sales representatives who had completed the training program, twenty met the selection criteria and were thus highly possible success cases. I randomly selected five of these reps to interview and sent each a note to schedule my talk with them. Interestingly enough, I had only to conduct two interviews to find out everything that I needed to know.

Here is what I learned in my very first two interviews, with two sales reps whom I will call Pat and Lynn:

Pat, I discovered, had used the training brilliantly and was highly successful in landing new accounts and in increasing sales volume of especially profitable products. It was easy, as well, to see why Pat's training had been so successful. Many organizational factors and actions virtually assured success. For example: Pat's experience in the training actually began well before the training itself with a sales manager who had taken great pains to assure that there would be a benefit to the training. The manager, for instance, had met with Pat and discussed new sales goals, then had personally enlisted the help of the training department to assure that the training program was aligned with these goals. Further, Pat had very clear performance objectives, and there was a system for providing regular feedback and coaching, if needed. Also, the training was scheduled well in advance, and Pat was able to clear calendar events to assure the least disruption and the greatest convenience. Finally, after the training, Pat and the manager had a number of meetings and co-calls wherein the new methods were tried out, assessed, tried out more, and eventually refined into a seamless application process.

Lynn, on the other hand, had made no use of the training whatsoever. Again, the causes for this were not hard to discern. Lynn had been forced to attend the training on very short notice and at considerable personal expense. The worst of these disruptions was that Lynn had to cancel already scheduled plans to take an eleven-year-old son on a day-long birthday outing—with six of his friends, no less—to a professional baseball game. To make matters poignantly worse, Lynn had missed the previous two birthday celebrations for this same child, being out of town on sales business. But Lynn, under pressure, went to the training, and obviously (as I already knew) did very well. On returning, however, Lynn encountered no support at all for using the training and soon gave up after some frustrating initial attempts. There were, for example, no measurement methods in place to use the new sales tools, and the manager was unable or unwilling to provide coaching. At the time of the interview, Lynn was working on a new job résumé and was seeking a new job with a different company. Prospects were grim, however. Lynn admitted that, despite the frustration with the current position, it would probably be prudent (though not inspiring) to stick with the current job for the next twelve years until retirement was an option. Curiously, Lynn still agreed that the training was the best ever experienced and planned to include it in the résumé as having completed it successfully (Lynn had earned the top mastery score!), which might be a favorable factor in the new job search.

I left this second interview feeling nearly as depressed as poor Lynn, but I knew that I had discovered some key and profound truths and that I was very close to being able to make some useful recommendations to my client. First, though, I wanted to confirm that I hadn't happened, by chance, to just stumble across an odd-ball pair of sales reps. I had selected my interviewees at random, but still, there was a chance that chance alone had biased my sampling. I asked for permission to make contact with several more sales reps. I sent a note to another random sample from those who scored highest on the test and asked them just one question: How much are you using the new tools and methods? The answers I got back were equally enlightening—less than half of them were using the methods; the rest reported as little use as Lynn.

Here is what I concluded:

- *The training was probably as good, if not better, than it needed to be. It taught the skills well. I told my client that no revisions at all were needed to the sales rep training itself.*
- *Success, when defined as actual usage of the learned skills, was largely determined by what happened before and after the training. This was probably more important that the quality of the training and the inherent abilities of the sales reps (all of them were veteran performers with good records). If the trainee came from and returned to a supportive performance environment, there was a high probability of success. If the trainee came from and returned to a "toxic" (or at best a benignly negligent) performance environment, failure was likewise assured.*
- *The company needed more trainees like Pat and fewer like Lynn. To get them, it needed more managers to behave like Pat's manager and fewer to behave like Lynn's manager. I suggested that they bolster the sales rep training with a determined initiative to help managers make better use of the training and provide the correct support, both before and after, which would assure success.*

Finally, I concluded that I had stumbled on a new way to do evaluation. I learned more from talking to a highly successful, and a highly unsuccessful, trainee than I typically learned in far more complex and methodologically sophisticated measurement initiatives. But I had gotten lucky and found by chance the very best, and worst, success cases from this training. How much more interesting and useful this could be, I thought, if I could find these best and worst cases on purpose, then learn from them! This helped me figure out that a brief survey to locate potential successes could be helpful and that I needed a picture of what I was looking for at the same time—an "impact model." I was on my way.

3.

Focusing and Planning a Success Case Study

Although there is a common overall framework for the Success Case Method, each particular study has its own unique purpose and context; in this respect, there are as many variants as there are Success Case studies. The aim of this chapter is to provide guidance in thinking through all of the particular requirements that will shape the study to be sure that it will be effective—providing stakeholders with the information they need and providing useful answers to the questions that constitute the purpose.

As noted in the preceding chapter, there are several considerations and decisions that must be made en route to planning a useful and efficient Success Case study. These are:

1. Clarify and define the purpose of the study
2. Review the information needs, interests, and concerns of key stakeholders
3. Define the program or initiative that is the object of the SC study
4. Identify the people in the program who are the focus of the SC study and clarify any necessary sampling requirements
5. Decide how long to wait after the innovation to search for success data
6. Specify the time frame for completion of the study
7. Clarify the key resources (funding and other) that are available for investment in the study
8. Create a design for the study that will accomplish its key purposes within the resources and other constraints you have identified

Note that these considerations are not necessarily pursued in a stepwise, linear fashion. The overall aim of this first major SCM step is to accomplish this eighth consideration: to create a study design that will accomplish the key purposes for the study. All of the other considerations in the list interact with one another to shape the study, and discussion of one consideration inevitably leads to the necessity of modifying understanding of another consideration. The initial understanding of purpose, for instance, may need to be limited to accommodate the resources that are available for the study. Or, likewise, discussions with stakeholders may surface a time limitation that the study must accommodate, which will in turn delimit the scope of the study to a particular portion of the program being investigated, unless an increase in resources can be negotiated.

1. Clarify and Define the Purpose of the Study

An SC study has the general intent of finding out how well some program or initiative is working. But why is this important? This "deeper dive" into the intent helps to clarify and define the purpose to frame and shape the SC study. In fact, the clarification of the purpose for the study can lead to a decision that the SCM is not the best approach. The SCM is good for some evaluation purposes, but not others.

If, for example, it is important to determine precisely how many people are making use of an innovation, or exactly how many people have completed or benefited from a program, the SC approach is not useful. The SC approach focuses on just a few—the most and least successful participants—to understand and document their success (or lack of it). When the central purpose is to gain a precise estimate of total numbers of people who are benefiting, or to determine the breadth of benefit for each of several demographic categories of participants, the more usual quantitative survey methods should be used. Even in these cases, however, it could be useful to "tack on" an SC study to a more exhaustive and comprehensive survey. That is, one could conduct a comprehensive survey, then follow up just a few successful and unsuccessful participants. On occasion, we have completed such "hybrid" studies for clients who would like precise information about program range and breadth but also want to illustrate successes with a few cases described in depth.

Here are some other purposes for which a Success Case approach normally would not be the best approach. Do not use the SCM when it is important to:

- Know how the typical or average participant feels or performs
- Gather opinions from all participants about a program regarding its usefulness, its strengths, and so forth
- Determine how many people in total, or numbers of people in certain categories, have participated in or are completely engaged in using all or parts of a program
- Determine the mean (average) amount of participation, benefit, usage, or so forth of a new innovation
- Track usage trends and patterns over time

The purposes listed are representative but not exhaustive of instances where the SCM would not be the right approach. Notice that the purposes for which the SCM is not suitable all require that data should be gathered from or about all participants in an initiative. When precise information about everyone is needed, or when central tendency means and averages are called for, the SCM is not an appropriate choice.

There are, of course, many instances when the SCM approach is a good one. Some of the key objectives that the SCM has been effectively used to address are:

- Estimating the ROI (return on investment) of a program
- Guiding revisions to improve a program by figuring out what is working and what is not
- Documenting the actual nature of benefits that program participants have experienced
- Deciding whether a pilot or "test" program is good enough to be rolled out to larger audiences

- Helping leaders decide whether to support a program by showing them what worthwhile outcomes (if any) it is achieving
- Documenting the actual impact of a program to allay (or confirm!) the concerns of skeptics and "nay-sayers"
- Creating examples of success for use in marketing a program or otherwise convincing others of its value
- Figuring out exactly how people are using some innovation when its actual potential is unknown
- Refining and improving a program based on the experience of those who are actually using it
- Accelerating a change initiative by demonstrating the success of early adopters to recalcitrant and other latter participants
- Helping managers identify and understand the factors that they need to manage (through, for example, coaching and feedback) if they wish their employees to make successful use of an innovation or program

The list is of generic, major objectives and applications. In practice, each was further refined in interaction with key stakeholders. In working with training leaders in a company to evaluate their training program in emotional intelligence, for example, the general purpose for our SC study was to assess and document impact. There was general agreement, based on sporadic anecdotal evidence, that the program was probably useful and was helping people achieve worthwhile results. There were questions, however, about whether the actual impact of the program was really worthwhile in light of what the overall business was hoping to achieve. Senior leaders wanted to make a decision about how, and how much, to support maintenance or extension of the program. As we talked with key stakeholders about their interests and concerns, more detail about their information needs and expectations emerged.

Thus, the study requirements became further understood until we reached agreement that it needed to address the following questions:

- What, if any, specific applications of emotional intelligence training outcomes are employees making?
- How do these applications differ according to types of employees (e.g., advisors, field office managers, and regional executives)?
- What is the business value of the applications?
- What factors are supporting and inhibiting the application of training outcomes?
- What suggestions can be made to improve the impact of the training?

Initial understandings of purposes are always liable to be further refined and developed by the key stakeholders. Thus, it is relevant now to turn to that consideration.

2. Review the Information Needs, Interests, and Concerns of Key Stakeholders

A stakeholder is, as the name implies, a person or group who holds a "stake" in the program being studied—a person who cares about, or whose welfare could be affected by, whether the program works or not. This will include those who will use the results of the SC study, such as program sponsors and managers. Program "owners," such as those who lead or otherwise help to implement the program or innovation being studied, are also stakeholders, as the results of the study may influence decisions about their program, even to the point of deciding that it may be a candidate for termination. Stakeholders also include program participants. If they are getting any benefits, then they probably hope that the program will survive. If the program is not doing them any good, then they would probably prefer that their time not be wasted with it. Potentially, of course, almost everyone is a stakeholder. Nonparticipants, for example, might be able to have access to some other resources if the program being studied were expanded, or replaced with, something else. To be practical, though, we identify and communicate with the major and obvious stakeholders.

Identifying stakeholders is a crucial step in any evaluation effort. Once a study is underway, and certainly after it is concluded, it is difficult to change it to accommodate the interests of a stakeholder who was overlooked. It is also common that an ignored or overlooked stakeholder emerges later in a study to undermine the study or discredit its findings.

●————————————————————————————●

An Overlooked Stakeholder Rears His Head—Ugly!

I wondered why enrollments in our West Virginia program meeting were far below what we expected. It was, after all, the national debut of our Evaluation Training Consortium (ETC), a large federally funded program intended to help special education professionals learn about and use program evaluation methods and tools to improve their program effectiveness. We were proud of our marketing efforts and had been encouraged by a warm response from all those to whom we had talked in the months prior to our session. But here we were just six weeks away from the meeting, and not only had the anticipated enrollments not materialized but several early enrollees had called to cancel. I was worried. I had inherited leadership of the program after the untimely death of my doctoral advisor and knew that many in the funding agency were skeptical of my ability to run this large and expensive program.

One of the registrants who had canceled was a previous acquaintance. I called her, and after some heartfelt begging, she agreed to tell me what was really going on in West Virginia. A man of whom I had not heard, but who happened to be the previous (now retired) director of special education in the state, had recently made a presentation at a faculty retirement dinner held in the state capitol. At the reception prior to his talk, he had made it a point to tell everyone who would listen that he had heard from his insider friends in the federal government that this federal "shindig" that I was running was already a dead program and was slated to be discontinued. Unbeknown to me (because he was long retired and not on my list of key contacts and influential people), this gentleman considered himself the "grandfather" of special education in the state. As he had not been invited to my program meeting, it thus could not be important. He was miffed, and right or wrong, he had made it a personal mission to undermine my program. I immediately called him at his home and apologized for my oversight. We talked a long time, and he recounted the days of his youthful professional start and some of the mistakes he had made, not unlike mine. We agreed that he would be the guest convenor of my meeting and that we would co-host a cocktail reception the evening before. Lo and behold, enrollments bounced back. The meeting was a success, and I went on to win renewed funding and lead the ETC for eleven more years. More importantly, I came into possession of a good story that I have told to many students about why stakeholder analysis is important.

●───●

Evaluations are meant to have a consequence, such as making a decision to extend a program, support it, refine it, or even terminate it. Because these consequences affect people, sometimes in dramatic and profound ways, evaluators have an ethical responsibility to thoroughly identify stakeholders and understand and consider their needs and interests. Though it may not be possible to accommodate the interests of all stakeholders, decisions to not accommodate interests must be made intentionally and with due consideration, not by default or oversight.

The number of stakeholders, the interests they represent, and the intensity of their interest in the study depends on the scope and purpose of the study. If, for example, the study is brief and has a very limited scope, the range and interests of stakeholders may be relatively limited. In one study, for instance, we followed up with only three users of a new employee development planning system in a small company; these were the first few managers to report that they had used the new process and materials in meetings with their employees. The purpose of this very limited study was only to find out how well the materials worked, whether the employees in the discussion felt successful, and what revisions the process or materials might need. Stakeholders in this case were the human resources team who had created the development planning process, the president of the company who would decide whether to recommend that the system be adopted, the consultant who assisted, the initial actual users, and the potential users (all managers and employees). Thus, the human resources team was involved in planning the study as was the consultant. The president was informed that a field trial was taking place and was assured that she would receive a report. All employees were informed that a new system was under consideration in an all-company email and were asked to register their concerns (if any) with the human resources team leader. The consultant helped plan the study. The report on the trial, and the decisions made to change the materials, was archived in the company's information system and was thus available to any employee.

In another study we had to more carefully and formally involve stakeholders, and their somewhat conflicting interests had to be resolved before we could proceed. This was an evaluation of management training provided to a worldwide staff of branch office managers in a large international child welfare and development agency. The training investment in this case exceeded $12 million over the preceding three years, and the agency board was considering a decision to renew, or terminate, the training contract with an outside provider.

- The provider of the training wanted to protect their stake in the program and have their contract renewed. Thus, they wanted the evaluation to be as broad as possible and include all of the variables most likely to have led to positive outcomes.

- The agency board, on the other hand, wanted a quick study that would be accurate, but also as cheap as possible. They had already felt they spent too much on the training and did not want to throw much more money into an evaluation.

- Field managers were accountable for branch office results and stood to be terminated if their offices underperformed. Historically, very little training had been provided, thus they were intensely concerned that they might lose their access to training. They supported the continuation of the training and in fact wanted more training and other support that had even the slightest chance of helping them succeed.

- Field employees, on the other hand, were jealous of the training opportunities their leaders received, because it enabled them to travel away from the harsh field conditions and increased their workload during the absence of the managers.

In this study, we spent several weeks meeting with representatives of the various factions and interests, seeking to understand their concerns and demonstrate a commitment to their interests. Several design options were forwarded for consideration, then reviewed by the factions before we reached agreement on an approach. Some of the board members wanted us just to do a survey because it would be cheap. Others (quite rightfully) said they would not trust any survey results, because the field managers would say anything to get to keep their training access. We finally agreed on a rigorous Success Case study of a few representative field offices in different parts of the world. If the training were working in these tough-to-manage offices, it would stand a chance of winning support for continuation. The study did indeed surface compelling benefits. This helped the board reach a satisfactory decision: to continue the training but in a form that would be briefer, less expensive, and more targeted to specific and unique field office needs. In this case, stakeholder identification and consideration was probably the most complex challenge for the study. Once we had everyone in agreement, the rest of the study was really quite easy!

3. Define the Program or Initiative that Is the Object of the SC Study

This sounds like a very obvious and simple directive. Indeed it is obvious, but it is rarely quite as straightforward and simple as it sounds. For example, consider the instance of our assessment of the emotional intelligence training: In this study, we were asked to use the SCM to assess the impact of the "emotional intelligence training program." One of the first questions we needed to resolve was this: Exactly what is the "program"? Emotional intelligence training was deeply embedded in this company and consisted of several formal and informal training interventions. There were also many other "one-off" sorts of presentations, orientations, and training sessions that the corporate training office had provided when none of the standard offerings were convenient. Finally, there were several self-instructional and videotaped modules, as well as a number of brief brochures and other written resources that employees could use in a variety of combinations. We decided, after considerable discussion with stakeholders, that for our evaluation purposes the "program" would be defined as three separate elements, each for a different audience: (a) the one-day session for financial advisors; (b) the five-day workshop for executives; and (c) the three-day office workshop. Anyone else who participated in some other form of emotional intelligence training was not considered to be a participant in "the program." These more formal sessions had involved large numbers of participants and could be reasonably expected to have been largely the same regardless of how many times or in how many places they had been provided. With the "one-off" sessions, there was no assurance of sameness among them so we could not reasonably consider them a "program."

Nontraining interventions determining what is or is not a "program" is likewise problematic. Consider, for example, the case of the company that provided laptop computers to its sales staff. At first consideration, this would seem to be simple—the program is the distribution of the laptops. But software bundles differed among the laptop distribution phases so some sales reps got one version of software and others another. Then we discovered that the laptops themselves differed in some key respects. Some had, for instance, internal versus external modems, thus making them easier to use in different settings. Further some sales reps received training along with their laptops and others did not. In some sales districts, the district managers received training and their own laptops; in others they got only the laptops; and others got nothing at. For some of these differences, we could simply treat them as contextual variables, accounting for their effects as we explored success cases. However, our stakeholders felt some of the laptop distribution was too hastily done or without adequate support to actually be considered a part of the "program." In the end, the laptop distribution program was determined to be constituted of a combination of: (1) a laptop with a specific software bundle that was (2) provided in districts where the managers had similar laptops, and (3) where the laptops were also accompanied by either training or support documentation.

The point of all this is that the program must indeed be defined in clear terms that delimit—for all to understand—what is and what is not the program. Only then should the evaluation planning move forward to the next, related step, of determining the appropriate numbers and sample of participants.

4. Identify the People in the Program Who Are the Focus of the SC Study and Clarify Any Necessary Sampling Requirements

This step actually continues the determination of defining the program, except that now we must delimit the program to only some particular subset of participants. In one case, for example, we included in the evaluation only those participants who (1) worked in the continental United States and (2) had participated in an innovation within a given eight-month period. The restriction to the continental United States assured that we could reach participants by email, and the restriction to a certain time frame was made because the program had undergone a revision just prior to that, thus the earlier versions would not be comparable. We further restricted the population to only regional executives, branch office managers, and repair technicians, as these were the principal target groups for whom business value from the innovation could be reasonably expected and was promoted. Employees who worked in the central corporate office in staff functions were not included, nor were those who held jobs other than those listed, as these were too infrequently represented in the company to constitute any sort of critical mass.

In an evaluation of the deployment of an individual development planning system for a large oil company, it was necessary to carefully define particular employees who would be included. In a generic sense, the target population was all managers and all of their employees. In discussions with stakeholders, however, we learned that it would not be wise to treat the company as a single entity. Recent acquisitions of oil distributors had occurred, and the acquired companies had to abandon the development planning system they already used. Thus, we were careful to include separate samples of employees from each of the acquired companies, as we were quite sure that we would discover, and want to analyze and report on, the differences in adoption of the system that might be encountered. Similarly, senior human resources executives informed us that some of the refinery operations in New Jersey represented work environment cultures very different from the cultures in corporate sales and support locations. Refineries were infamous for—and proud of—their roughhouse, "dog eat dog" approach to work. If we were to combine data from these cultures with the milder and more human-relations sensitive samples from corporate offices, we would mislead ourselves as to how well and completely the system was being adopted. Thus we ended up with several separate samples so we could track and compare adoption across several company organizational units and look for success cases in each.

Readers should note that separation of a population into different samples might entail, de facto, the subdivision of the SC study into several SC studies. That is, a separate survey may be used for each sample, and separate success case instances may be developed for each sample. This is tantamount to implementing several separate SC studies, which of course will add to cost and complexity.

5. Decide How Long to Wait After the Innovation to Search for Success Data

This step actually continues the specification of who is "in" and who is "out" of a study. That is: Is there is a time frame that is used to define the program and participant parameters that define inclusion in, or exclusion from, the study? You have to wait for some period of time after an innovation is introduced until you can expect it to have impact. Then, you also cannot study participation too long after a program has been in place, as people are likely to forget what they did and what they used or even if they participated or not.

In one study, for example, we determined that to be included in the study, participants must have received their support tool package (1) no later than in the past eight months, and (2) no earlier than in the past six weeks. One intended usage of the tools, for example, was to help install a client computer system. Technicians did not have a chance to do this on a daily basis. Customer service data showed that a six-week time frame should be sufficient to have at least one opportunity to work on an installation. In other words, our thinking went, if they hadn't made use of the tools in at least the first six weeks after receiving them, chances are they were not going to try them at all. On the other hand, if we went back in time more than eight months, their memory of which tools they had used or not used would be unreliable, as there were several resources provided to them.

In another case, we were evaluating the installation of new telephone call handling methods in a service call center. We expected that the innovation should have been used in the very first calls received. In this instance, the innovation was installed during one week. We began to look for impact the very next week.

The timing issue is the same, whether the intervention being studied is an organizational change, a technological innovation, a training program, or some other initiative. Here are the defining criteria for deciding how soon to measure and how far back in time to measure:

- *Don't evaluate too soon.* The intervention must have had time to have an effect. People must be given some realistic time frame within which they will encounter enough opportunities to apply or experience the intervention with success. In other words, success must be given a chance.
- *Don't wait too long or sample participants too far back in time.* The intervention cannot be so old as to be lost in memory or otherwise likely to be confused with other interventions and ini-

tiatives that will make recalled experiences too unreliable. If you sample too far back in time, participants may not accurately recall exactly what they did, what they used, what they did not use, and so forth. We rarely sample participation for more than one year after an innovation is introduced.

6. Specify the Time Frame for Completion of the Study

It is always necessary to identify any time constraints on the study, especially the deadline by which the study must be complete and a final report prepared and submitted. A caution here: Be careful in making promises about time parameters. There are two aspects of an SC study that are notoriously difficult to manage. One is the time people will take in completing and returning a survey. We almost always allow at least two weeks after the date of distribution for the completion and return of surveys. The second aspect of the study that can take a long time is scheduling and completing Success Case interviews. The people you identify for Success Case interviews may be extremely busy, and it can be difficult to get even the forty-five minutes or so needed for the interview to be scheduled. Then, inevitably, some will cancel the initial interview date and need to reschedule.

An Elusive Marketing Vice President

The first step in our study was to interview the VP of marketing, as he would help us define the impact that was most expected and needed by the company. Only after we had talked to him could we proceed to survey and interview marketing representatives. Our first appointment was scheduled to take place in the Toronto office of the company while I was there meeting with their human resources department on another matter. The VP's secretary left me a message that we would have to reschedule. The next meeting was set for a week later to take place by phone while the VP had a one-hour layover in Chicago on his way west. But his flight was delayed and in fact he had no time for our call. The third attempt was two weeks after that, and again we were foiled, this time by an emergency board meeting to discuss a looming company merger. The fourth attempt likewise got derailed. Just a matter of days after that, I got a call from the secretary as I was making a breakfast bowl of oatmeal. The VP had to stay at home that morning to meet a washer repairman who was notoriously hard to reach. Could I call him on his cell phone at home while he waited by his back door? You bet! I did, we talked, his washer got fixed (my oatmeal got cold, but so it goes), and the project was on its way. Six weeks behind schedule, but on its way.

It is not unusual for us to schedule one full month to complete SC interviews, even when we have only a few to complete. But these are the sorts of scheduling constraints that any investigator in organizational settings are familiar with, and common sense and good project management principles should be the rule of the day.

7. Clarify the Key Resources (Funding and Other) that Are Available for Investment in the Study

Again, this is a familiar action for anyone who plans and implements projects in organizations. Almost always, it is necessary to revisit and renegotiate either the scope of the study or the resources available for it. Inevitably, you will find that some initially desired objective of the study must be limited to accommodate the resources available. It will be useful to point out, however, the particular cost elements and risks that are unique to SC studies.

Typically, the most expensive and time-consuming portions of an SC study are the survey, the interviews to explore, and documenting the success cases. Of these two major portions of the SCM study, the survey is usually the lesser expensive and time-consuming process. Sometimes a formal written survey is not used at all. That is, sometimes we can identify potential success cases without a survey, tapping into the "grapevine" or otherwise asking for referrals and references. However, most SC studies employ a written survey, some more extensive than others. Later, in Chapter 5, we present and discuss the survey process in more detail. At this point readers are cautioned to carefully consider the survey process that will be used and be sure it is within the budget available. Email methods make the overall survey process far more efficient and cost-effective (assuming that the software and systems are already in place). When paper and pencil surveys are used, costs are significantly increased. Likewise, the complexity of the survey and sampling methods, as they increase, will drive costs up.

The interview portion of the study is typically the greatest cost factor. Adding more respondents to the survey adds little cost, especially when email is used, but adding more success cases for interviewing adds directly and proportionally to costs. It costs relatively little to develop an interview plan and protocol, and once developed it is reusable. However, if a client wants to document eight cases instead of four success cases, the costs will roughly double. Interviewing is time-consuming and almost always takes longer than expected due to interrupted interviews, cancellations, false starts, and so forth.

When budgeting for interviews, we typically estimate that it will take us three hours of work to complete each forty-five-minute interview (though I have recounted the story of the six-week interview, so beware). This will include time for preparation for the interview (reviewing the interviewee's survey, for example), making the telephone connection, conducting the interview, and writing up the notes afterward. This three-hour estimate also includes a factor for cancellations and rescheduling, which often occur with interviews.

The interview process also takes the highest level of professional expertise. Success Case interviews are relatively open-ended and require an experienced and expert interviewer who is capable of understanding complex phenomena and can subtly redirect responses, detect falsehoods, and so forth. Chapter 6 provides more detail on the interview process and will be helpful in thinking through cost needs for a particular study.

8. Create a Design for the Study that Will Accomplish Its Key Purposes Within the Resources and Other Constraints You Have Identified

There are as many particular SC plans and designs as there are instances of SC studies. Each study follows the same overall conceptual framework, but each has to be adapted and customized to fit the particular needs and constraints of any given context. Although there is a general framework for an SC study, there is no particular "cookbook" method we can share to provide a reader with each nuance and detail of his or her particular study. It is probably helpful, however, to review some typical SC examples.

To this end, following in Table 3.1 are a number of representative examples of SC studies we have conducted, each addressing a different purpose. This is not an exhaustive list; we have used SCM approaches for more purposes than these and readers will discover additional uses. However, the list is representative of the uses for which my colleagues and I have found the SCM to be helpful, and it serves as a useful guide to understand the breadth of potential applications for the SCM approach.

Table 3.1 shows the following information for each study example: The left-hand column provides a brief overview of the program that was the focus of the study. The middle column explains the intent of the study (what the client needed the study to accomplish). The right-hand column provides a brief summary of the particular design we used to address the client's need(s).

Table 3.1: How the Success Case Study Was Designed to Meet Some Representative Client Needs for Several Different Programs

The Program	The SCM Intent	The Design
A large telecommunications company that had invested in a mandatory supervisor training program	*Resolving concerns about impact:* Senior leadership wanted some hard evidence about the program's impact.	• Selected random samples of training participants from each major business unit and functional department to be sure to represent all supervisors.
	Senior managers were reluctant to send their people to something that doesn't pay off, especially as personnel shortages have stressed workloads.	• Sent a survey to the participants, asking them to note which (from a list) supervisory actions they had tried and what beneficial results, if any, had been achieved.
		• Interviewed and documented successes in each of several major categories (e.g., using the skills to avert a lawsuit, using the skills to increase production).

Table 3.1: How the Success Case Study Was Designed to Meet Some Representative Client Needs for Several Different Programs *(continued)*

The Program	The SCM Intent	The Design
A software company that had invested in some new product demonstration presentation graphics and equipment.	*Modeling and motivating successful applications:* Some sales reps seem to be making good use of the materials, but a large majority appear to not be using it at all. They hope that demonstrating some of the successes will stimulate others to try it, eventually getting a lot of people to use it, thus increasing sales.	• Sent an email survey to all sales reps asking who had tried the materials, and what success, if any, they had experienced. • Identified the most successful sales reps. • Conducted an email interview with these reps and documented their success. • Constructed a report that showed exactly how the materials had been used and how much success was achieved. The report was then captured in a brief file, which was forwarded to all of the reps and their district managers; it included specific guidance on how to get similar results. • The "Success Case" reps were made available (online) as resource "coaches" to help anyone who might ask.

Table 3.1: How the Success Case Study Was Designed to Meet Some Representative Client Needs for Several Different Programs *(continued)*

The Program	The SCM Intent	The Design
An automobile company that was trying out an expensive new satellite television network for delivering brief training and technical assistance programs to dealerships nationwide	*Extending program benefits to more users:* The expensive system was being underutilized by most dealerships. The client particularly wanted to demonstrate to dealers who are not using the service that it can pay off and help them adopt some of the "best practices" that other dealerships have employed.	• Identified a stratified sample of dealerships that would represent major dealer categories (e.g., large urban, large suburban, rural, and so forth), who also had participated in the service. • Sent a survey to these selected dealers asking how much success, if any, they could attribute to their participation in the service. • Selected a small sample of "extremes"—those who claimed a lot, or virtually no, success. • Conducted follow-up interviews by phone with selected dealership personnel to explore, verify, and document the successes. • Prepared a report that highlighted the range and nature of success the program could lead to. The report also pinpointed the particular actions (e.g., giving time off to participate) that dealers who had experienced success used, so that others who wanted to achieve the same sort of results would know what else they had to do.

Table 3.1: How the Success Case Study Was Designed to Meet Some Representative Client Needs for Several Different Programs (continued)

The Program	The SCM Intent	The Design
A government agency that has installed some new client management software in some of its branch offices	*Estimating ROI (return on investment) to make a program roll-out decision:* There is an interest in providing the new software and processes to other branches. The central administration wants to see ROI evidence to help make the roll-out decision.	• Identified successful applications of the software and calculated the value of its application in each of three categories: • Serving more clients per day • Reducing errors in client processing • Decreasing the amount of management time needed to oversee the process • Conducted a survey that asked for reports of application of any of these uses. • Selected several success cases from respondents and interviewed them to validate and verify usage and cost-savings. • Translated these outcomes into dollar-value estimates that were then compared to costs. (The results showed that program benefits could deliver considerably more value than the cost of the innovation.)

Table 3.1: How the Success Case Study Was Designed to Meet Some Representative Client Needs for Several Different Programs *(continued)*

The Program	The SCM Intent	The Design
A consulting firm that sells online coaching services	*Marketing a service to skeptical prospects:* Sales reps reported some initial successes. The company wanted to document these so that the "stories" of success could be used to market the service to other companies. The aim was to provide evidence to potential but skeptical buyers that this sort of service can really work.	• Surveyed coaches to find out which of them reported the greatest success with their clients. • Chose three success cases that represented the major categories of clients the firm worked with (high tech, manufacturing, healthcare) and documented these, showing especially the business results that clients had achieved as a result of the coaching services. • Built the Success Case stories into marketing materials.

Table 3.1: How the Success Case Study Was Designed to Meet Some Representative Client Needs for Several Different Programs *(continued)*

The Program	The SCM Intent	The Design
A large computer company that conducted expensive residential training courses for service technicians	*Figuring out how to get more impact:* The company was receiving conflicting information about the effectiveness of a very expensive technical maintenance training. Cost-cutting pressures were high, and the company had to determine quickly what about the program was working as well as whether and how it could be made more efficient.	• Used a survey to identify extreme samples of successful applications of the training. • Identified samples of those participants who were not using the training and discovered that although many users were very successful and achieved dramatic impact, a shocking proportion of participants were not using the training. • Identified several key factors (after digging deep) that the company could better manage (e.g., trainee selection) to improve the proportion of successful trainees.

Table 3.1: How the Success Case Study Was Designed to Meet Some Representative Client Needs for Several Different Programs *(continued)*

The Program	The SCM Intent	The Design
A financial services company had invested a lot of money over the years in training its employees to use emotional intelligence skills	*Estimating "unrealized" impact:* The training department needed to decide (1) if there was additional impact of value that the training could achieve, and if so (2) whether and how the training could be revised to achieve greater impact for more people.	• We posited several applications of the training that were likely to be creating valuable impact • We used a survey to identify representative Success Case examples (in each of the Success Case categories) from extreme groups of people getting a great deal of value to those receiving no value at all. • Analyzed survey data to identify proportions of participants who could have, but did not, use the training to receive value. • Estimated the amount of value that would accrue if more of these nonusers were to use the training (it was substantial). • Searched (through interviews) specifically for workplace factors that were consistently reported to impede usage of the training. • Pinpointed the major workplace factors that could be influenced through more training or better management of training processes. • Made suggestions for changing the training and for changing how supervisors managed access and application of the training. • Estimated the value of each of these changes by making conservative estimates of the results that greater training could lead to.

Again, readers should note that these SC examples are illustrative only and do not represent an exhaustive list of the ways in which SC studies can be put to work. It should, however, be apparent that any SC study has to be designed with its own unique purposes and constraints in mind. The SC Method is based on a general conceptual framework (inquiry into extreme groups and storytelling), but is not a cookie-cutter procedure. Each SC study is unique and adapts an approach that will work best for a particular setting and purpose.

4

Envisioning Success: Creating an Impact Model

Creating the impact model is a relatively brief but highly important step in planning an SC study. The impact model is a carefully articulated and concise "forecast" of what the most successful performance might be expected to look like if the program we are studying is accomplishing what its stakeholders hope it should. In other words, the impact model answers the question: If things were working well, what would be happening?

The impact model serves as the basis for the survey and for the questions that will be asked during Success Case interviews. Because the survey portion of the study is intended to discover those participants who report the greatest success, it is necessary to know what success would look like so that the survey "knows what it is looking for." Likewise, the interviews are intended to describe and document successful applications in detail, thus the questions asked during the interview must be aimed in the right direction.

This chapter presents and discusses several examples of impact models used in actual SC studies. By reviewing these examples, readers will develop an understanding of what an impact model is. Following the presentation and discussion of examples, the author provides guidance in how an impact model can be created and validated. In some SC studies, it is necessary to create only a brief and superficial impact model; in other instances, a thoroughly detailed impact model is required. The chapter closes with a discussion of the situations in which more, or less, detail is needed, and it provides guidelines for making this key decision.

The Impact Model

Table 4.1 provides an example of an impact model that was developed for "Core, Inc." (a fictitious name for an actual telecommunications company with whom we worked). Core, Inc. had begun a highly publicized and strategic supervisory support initiative intended to help the company achieve some critical business goals, especially focusing on retention of employees. Core had set aggressive global expansion goals and knew that their business strategy would be foiled if they lost employees to "raiders" from competitors (stealing employees from one's competitors was a rampant practice in the rapidly expanding dot.com era). The Core impact model represents the intended outcomes for the new supervisory support system, which included three key elements: (1) the adoption of a new performance management model that stressed coaching, (2) decentralization of human resources (HR) support through online access to HR forms, policies, and so forth, and (3) a mandatory training program for all supervisors.

Here are some important features of the impact model presented in Table 4.1 that are common to all impact models.

- The impact model is structured in table form with several columns.
- The column on the far left-hand side of the impact model represents capability in the form of the tools, knowledge, skill, and access that the new system intends to provide to supervisors.

- The far right-hand column of the impact model represents the critical overall business goals to which Core intended the new supervisory system to contribute.
- The middle columns (critical actions and key supervisor results) represent supervisors' job performance: the key behaviors and outcomes in which the new capability should be employed to help achieve the intended business goals.
- They highlight the "line of sight" that link an organizational initiative (in this case the new supervisory support system) to some overall business goals.
- They highlight the construct of the performance—actual behavior in key job tasks—that is the "channel" through which capability is transformed into results of value.
- They are brief and concise. They are strategic, not comprehensive. They typically include no more than five to seven entries per column, aiming to capture the most important few elements in each category.
- They communicate, in a nutshell, the essence of the "business case" for an initiative—how the capability produced in a new initiative can be used in actual performance to help achieve business goals.

FIGURE 4.1 Supervisory Support System Impact Model for Core Inc.

KEY KNOWLEDGE & SKILLS	CRITICAL ACTIONS	KEY SUPERVISORY RESULTS	CORE GOALS
Understand link between effective supervision and Core's strategic goals	Engage in frequent conversations with direct reports to understand business and personal goals	Attrition levels reduced within critical talent pools	Attract, develop and retain talent
Know how to access and use critical HR policies/forms/support to supervise effectively	Make accurate and timely access and referrals to HR resources to meet needs and interests of direct reports	Litigation costs and liability exposure reduced	Achieve sustainable growth by leveraging our economic investment in people through effective supervision
Leverage the diversity in a work group to create positive, effective work group	Systematically employ learning resources to develop talents of direct reports	Flexible/skilled/satisfied work force created	
Use listening skills to help people/teams resolve problems	Effectively employ performance management methods and tools to coach direct reports	Meet or exceed work unit performance goals	
Gain agreements to help others understand and make commitments	Reduce/resolve incidents that may threaten liability exposure before they erupt into serious problems		
Confront unmet needs to build accountability			
Provide feedback to coach others' performance and development			
Manage conflicts to keep team and individual relationships positive and business focused			

Core's Supervisor Effectiveness Evaluation

All impact models take a similar form to the model in Table 4.1, though each may employ different language to adhere to common usage in the client setting. For instance, what is called a "Key Result" on one impact model may be a "Performance Objective" on another, or a "Strategic Goal" in one client setting may be a "Corporate Imperative" in another. Regardless of the terms employed, however, the impact model must link the program or initiative to some longer-range and higher-level business goal or need, because it is the business outcomes that the initiative help address that determine the value of the initiative. And always, the middle portion of the impact model lists specific performance behaviors for teams or individuals.

The business goal to which the program is linked may be an overall organizational goal, or it may be the goal of a smaller organizational unit. This will depend on the nature and scope of the program for which you are planning an SC study. The evaluation of emotional intelligence training, for example, was an organization-wide initiative that involved many people in several roles. In this case, the program was intended to help achieve the organization's overall goals of customer retention, increasing sales, and so forth. In another case, however, the program studied may be limited to a smaller portion of the organization. In these instances, the entries in the farthest right-hand column may represent only work unit objectives. In any case, however, it is important to identify the business value of the performance identified in the middle of the model, whether this is represented by a small unit objective or the highest-level organizational goals, because this is the referent and determinant for the value of the program.

The Success Case approach seeks to tell stories about what those teams and individuals actually did to achieve success, thus the impact model should specify the precise sorts of behaviors for which the SC study will search. The most that a new initiative alone accomplishes immediately—whether it is provision of training, access to online resources, new technology, or new tools and methods—is only capability. Unless the capability introduced by the initiative is actually used by people in effective ways, then the initiative cannot produce value. Thus the SC approach, as operationalized in the impact model, must seek for and document the actual performance that did or did not take place.

Though performance—detailed analysis of exactly how capabilities are deployed in successful actions—is the focus of an SC study, the impact model always includes a denotation of the capabilities themselves. By identifying and listing the capabilities, we assure that others and we understand the logic of the overall program or intervention. Listing the separate capabilities also helps identify the intended applications to be sure that a key application is not overlooked. Finally, in analyzing SC data, we may find that a failure to achieve success was caused by a failure of capability rather than performance being blocked or inhibited by some organizational context factor such as a lack of an incentive. Listing key capabilities allows us to probe (in a survey or follow-up interview) on whether a failure to apply a program tool or method may be due to the fact that the person being studied never fully developed the capability in the first place. That is, if people were unable to do something because they lacked a key skill or knowledge, then it is clear that a success will not follow. Or, if a new tool was never made available at all, then it could not have been used.

Impact Model: The Beginning or the End?

Always, some form of impact model is created at the beginning of an SC study. The specificity of the impact model, however, is driven by the purpose of the study. Some SC studies are very open-ended, seeking to discover for the first time how a new initiative is, or is not, being used. That is, some organizational initiatives are quite open-ended, providing only some tools or skills that have the potential to be used in a number of ways, but not being prescriptive about how exactly they might be used. In these instances, the purpose of the Success Case study is, in large part, simply to discover and document successful practices, if any can be found.

Consider, for example, an initiative we studied many years ago in which public elementary students were provided (through an anonymous grant) with 35mm cameras; at the same time, their teachers were provided with brief training in teaching the pupils how to operate the cameras. But, how, when, where, and why the students might use the cameras was not predicted or prescribed. The assumption was that the cameras might get used in any number of ways, some of which might contribute to the longer-range goals of the school, to develop academic, personal growth, and citizenship skills. Table 4.2 shows the impact model for this very open-ended initiative.

Table 4.2 Impact Model for an Open-ended Initiative: Before the Study

Capability	Behavior	Results	Goals
How to load and unload film	?	?	Improved citizenship skills
How to operate basic camera controls			Improved academic performance
How to take pictures			Improved self-understanding

In this case, we first identified those students who claimed to have used their cameras in some ways that they believed were beneficial. In following up on these claims, we completed the central portion of the impact model, documenting a few quite productive uses for the cameras. Students had, we discovered, used the cameras in more common applications. The impact model in Table 4.3 shows the applications we were able to document.

Table 4.3
Impact Model for an Open-ended Initiative:
After the Study Capability Behavior Results Goals

Capability	Behavior	Results	Goals
How to load and unload film How to operate basic camera controls How to take pictures	Find and document instances of destructive behavior in and around the school (littering, for instance) Illustrate reports and papers Document unfair and biased social circumstances in the community (poverty, for instance)	Discussion and attention to more responsible behaviors Interest in journalistic endeavors Increased motivation for and interest in homework Greater awareness of and interest in correcting social conditions and inequities	Improved citizenship skills Improved academic performance Improved self-understanding

At the other end of the spectrum are organization change initiatives that are specific and prescriptive. In these cases, Success Case studies are focused on more highly intentional and specifically prescriptive behaviors, such as those seen in the Core, Inc., example provided in Table 4.1. In these instances, there is a high degree of specific intent, as the initiative has prescribed certain behavioral applications that are desired because they are believed to be the "right thing to do" to achieve some important business goals.

Many programs fall in a middle range. The example referred to earlier in which laptop computers were provided was relatively less determinate and prescriptive than the Core, Inc. example, but less open-ended than the students with cameras. The laptop program initiators were convinced that laptop technology could be leveraged in the sales process, and they had some categories of application in mind when they designed and presented the program. That is, they felt that laptops could be used to diagnose market opportunities, identify sales gaps with key and potential accounts, prepare sales calls, present materials, and so forth. But they did not present specific step-by-step examples and models, because none had yet been developed, nor did they want to delay the introduction of the technology to wait for development of these "cookbook" instructions; competitive pressures were high, and if they waited, too many sales opportunities would be lost to competitors. So, they quickly distributed the laptops and provided training in their operation to be sure that salespeople had the technical proficiency to operate their machines and software. But questions about exactly when and how to use the tools were left unanswered.

As it turned out, the early group of sales reps discovered some highly effective ways in which to use their laptops, and we carefully documented these through a brief SC study. These early applications served as guides and motivators to successive groups of users, and further SC studies provided increasingly detailed and richer stories of emerging uses.

In summary, some SC studies will require you to complete a fairly detailed and precise impact model at the beginning of the study so that you can assure that you understand how the program was intended to work and focus your inquiry on highly specific and precise actions and results. In other cases, you may begin the study with only a rudimentary and sketchy impact model. The level of specificity you need at the front end of the study will be driven entirely by the purpose for the study and the information needs of key stakeholders.

Creating Impact Models

The creation of an impact model is a relatively simple process once a purpose for the study has been agreed on, stakeholders have been identified, and the nature and scope (including program participants) of the program to be studied have been defined. Sources for information to complete the impact model vary according to the nature of the information sought. To identify business goals, for example, one needs access to senior leaders or at least to annual reports or other documents that will articulate important high-level goals. Information about program content and methods is typically available from those who planned and/or operate the initiative. Information about the roles and responsibilities of program participants may be available from program leaders, or it may be necessary to talk with some participants or their managers. In any case, SC study leaders will need to think through these they must access and other sources of information.

There is no particular order in which the information to complete the impact model should be pursued. That is, it is unimportant whether one starts with identifying business goals or specifying the particular capabilities (tools, methods, knowledge, and so forth) a program is intended to provide. The best rule of thumb is as follows: Start collecting information from whomever you are first in contact with and learn as much as you can from this source about any or all of the impact model information categories. Then, ask this person to whom else you can have access to get missing information. Continue this process until you have learned what you need to produce enough of an impact model to guide your study.

Table 4.4 provides some suggestions and guidance for completing each of the impact model information categories and will serve as a useful guide for readers.

Some Impact Model Examples

These closing pages of the chapter present some example impact models derived from a variety of different SC studies in which the author has been involved. A few explanatory notes to help readers understand the differences and nuances among the examples provided accompany each. Readers should note that some impact models employ different terms and language. Some even have different numbers of columns, again to reflect the peculiarities of different client contexts. Readers should also note that each impact model is based on the same fundamental structure; each always shows how some capability introduced by a particular program is intended to be applied (in job performance and results) to help achieve or contribute to some higher-level organizational goal.

Table 4.4

Tips for Completing an Impact Model

Impact Model	Category Suggestions
Business goals	Determine the highest-level goal that should be identified to justify and demonstrate the worth of the program (e.g., overall organization goal, division goal, work unit goal) then, interview program designers and/or leaders
	Ask questions of any available stakeholders
	Talk with senior executives and leaders
	Analyze business plans or strategic white papers
	Read annual reports
	Review the company's Web site
Program objectives and content (the capabilities it aims to create)	Observe the program in action (e.g., sit in on a training session)
	Review program materials
	Interview program designers and/or leaders
Critical actions (intended behavioral applications of the program capabilities)	Analyze the program objectives
	Review program case studies and examples
	Interview program designers and/or leaders
	Interview a few program participants
Key results (intended job/team application outcomes; performance objectives)	Visit some job sites and ask questions
	Review the performance appraisal forms or instruments the organization uses
	Interview a few managers of program participants
	Analyze the program objectives
	Review program case studies and examples
	Interview program designers and/or leaders
	Interview a few available program participants

State Family Welfare Agency Model

Table 4.5 shows the impact model for a state family welfare agency evaluation. This agency that provides services to needy families with dependent children introduced a new computerized system for conducting field office operations. The new hardware and software, provided along with training in its use, was intended to streamline operations, providing faster service, greater accuracy in reporting and accounting, and speedier referrals to coordinate cross-agency service provision. Because all field office job roles were impacted, we created impact models for each primary role (office director, administrative assistant, client services coordinator, and so on). Table 4.5 shows the impact model for only one of these roles: eligibility specialist.

This impact model is quite brief and focused as there were typically only a few key capabilities and critical applications of the new system that applied to each role. Because all of the roles were working in the same agency, the far right-hand column of the impact model was always the same, regardless of the role being modeled.

Table 4.5

Impact Model for Welfare Agency Eligibility Specialist Role

Capabilities	Critical Applications	Results	Agency Goals
Understanding of how new system ties to agency goals Ability to operate all software applications Ability to integrate system tools into agency processes	Use system to: Schedule interviews for prospective clients Create service file Determine eligibility Facilitate coordination of external agency services Update service files	Accurate and complete eligibility assessments Appropriate and complete client service assignments Accurate and up-to-date service files	Provide high-quality services quickly, accurately, completely, and efficiently (without rework) Improve satisfaction of clients, agency staff, and external agency stakeholders

Impact Model for Pharmaceutical Sales Reps Using Laptops

Table 4.6 shows the impact model for the sales representatives who were provided laptops for use in their sales efforts (an example referred to earlier in the book).

Table 4.6
Impact Model for Pharmaceutical Sales Representative Laptop Initiative

Capabilities	Critical Applications	Results	Business Goals
Sales reps with: Understanding of laptop potential Ability to operate laptop hardware Ability to use laptop software Access to company intranet	Analyze market area and identify high-leverage sales opportunities Analyze and interpret prescription-rate databases and apply to own market area Analyze current and potential accounts to identify sales and market-share growth opportunities Prepare customized sales presentations Conduct sales presentations with custom data and graphics Track sales performance and revise efforts as needed to keep strategic focus	Higher percentage of sales efforts dedicated to high-leverage strategic accounts Sales presentations customized to address account-specific opportunities Increased sales to key accounts Increased market share for high-leverage products in key accounts	Increased market share for key products Increased profits

Notice in this impact model that the "critical applications" listed are relatively general. This was the case because the initiative was brand new; although the planners of the laptop program had some general ideas about how the laptops might be used, they could not be at all specific about detailed steps the sales reps might employ for each application. This instance provides a good example of a program that was begun before there was detailed prescriptive guidance about how employees should use a new technology. The training that was provided to the sales reps consisted only of technical instruction in how to operate the computers and how to use the software. There was no training in exactly how to use the computers during a sales call, for instance, because no one knew yet how that might be done. It was up to the "pioneering" sales reps who first tried out the laptops to figure this out, and it was up to us—the SC study team—to document and describe their successful efforts so that others might learn from the "pioneers." But the business goals to which the computer program was to contribute were well-known and clearly specified.

Impact Model for a Beer Distributor

The impact model in Table 4.7 appears more complex, primarily because it depicts five job roles (rather than one, as in Tables 4.5 and 4.6). The beer distributor (which we have labeled with the fictitious name "Bulltoad Beer") impact model was developed as part of the assessment of a national marketing campaign. The national corporate marketing office for Bulltoad, one of the nation's largest brewers and distributors of beer, had initiated a national "freshness date" campaign (see discussion in Chapter One). This campaign, in which all containers of their product would have a prominently displayed date of production, was intended to increase sales and market share by providing the consumer with an assurance of the product's freshness. This new marketing initiative carried with it some relatively major and burdensome

Table 4.7

Impact Model: "Freshness Date" Marketing Campaign Training at Bulltoad Beer Distributors

Participants	Key Knowledge and Skills	Critical Applications	Key Results	Wholesaler Goals	Corporate Goals
Leadership team	Understanding of campaign goals, rationale, methods, and tools	Effectively communicate campaign requirements to distributorship staff	Distributorship staff able to effectively execute campaign process in compliance with corporate standards	Operations: • Reduce costs • Reduce shrinkage • Reduce downtime • Achieve corporate compliance targets Sales: • Increase volume • Increase market share • Increase retail shelf space (presence)	Increase profits through streamlined operations Increase market share Increase sales volume
Operation team leader	How to build team understanding and commitment How to delegate tasks to appropriate warehouse staff and sales team leaders How to provide coaching to teams How to use goal setting and coaching methods to accelerate sales performance	Empower teams to achieve all brewery requirements while meeting operations targets Coach new sales reps in campaign implementation Adhere to corporate standards for product handling in all distribution steps	Standardized operation and compliance as well as timely and effective achievement of distribution goals Effective application of campaign tools and methods in sales efforts Product freshness assured and compliance targets met		
Sales managers	How to use job aids for:				
Warehouse staff	• Correct product handling • Implementing compliance measures and reports				

product handling and storage requirements for distributors, principal among them was that the product would have to remain refrigerated at all times. Because the campaign required new sales and handling processes for distributors, it was accompanied by a training and awareness initiative that had been implemented for all distributors prior to the launch of the freshness date campaign. We had been engaged to help the brewery determine how much success distributors were achieving early in the campaign. The brewery was particularly anxious to identify the characteristics and factors that were associated with successful distributor compliance so that this information could be provided to distributors who were having problems—which happened to be a significant number, much to the frustration of the corporate leadership.

Note that this impact model is developed for five different distributor roles, showing at a very high level how each role was intended to use particular training to support the launch and implementation of the new campaign. This impact model was developed early in the evaluation to assure that we had a correct understanding of the overall initiative. Later, we would develop more detailed impact models for each of the roles because we needed to survey and develop success cases for each separate role.

Impact Model for Home Healthcare Services

This final impact model is the most complex yet because it shows how new system capabilities were to be used by three major staff roles. The setting for this SC study was a home healthcare services business that provided in-home temporary nursing services nationwide. The roles shown were employees who worked in a national service and call center unit that processed inbound service requests from the entire nation. New computer systems and automatic call distribution (800-number) technology made this business transformation possible, as all sales, scheduling for services, payments to nurses, and billing statements to customers were made from this single, highly automated service center.

The impact model in Table 4.8 depicts the three major staff roles: service representatives, account technicians, and shift supervisors (the call center operated on 24/7 shifts). In the second column, the key system capabilities for each role are shown. The next two columns show how the system capabilities were to be put into action by the employees as well as the expected key job results. The final three columns of the model show the process measures, business objectives for the call center, and overall strategic goals to which the jobs were to contribute.

Our SC inquiry was intended to assess how well the very earliest implementation efforts were working, hoping to identify especially quickly and accurately those workplace factors that were helping successful performers and hindering those who were less successful. Because the system was carefully planned in detail, the job behaviors in this impact model were very specific—unlike the previous impact model in Table 4.7—and represented a precise prescription for how employees were to use the new system methods and tools.

A Final Note on Impact Models

In most cases, impact models are not a final "deliverable" for an evaluation. In almost all instances, the purpose of the impact model is to help the evaluator (or evaluation team) understand and confirm their understanding of the program's intended applications and results. This understanding enables the researcher to focus the inquiry in the survey and interview phases of the evaluation.

In some cases, the impact model is a final result of the evaluation. This is the case when the purpose of the evaluation is to discover and document details of actual uses and applications such as in the "pioneering"

Table 4.8

Impact Model for Home Healthcare Service (HHS) Center Operations

Employees	Key System Capabilities	Critical Applications	Key Job Results	Process Measures	Business Objectives	Strategic Goal
Service Representatives	Customer service skills	Sell appropriate services	Sales of HHS services	One of eight calls converted to sales	Reduce daily sales outstanding to less than 3%	Achieve reputation as industry leader in • Total service quality • High-tech home care sales and quality
	Selling skills	Assign qualified caregivers to customers	Qualified caregivers assigned to client cases	Increase high-tech sales to 60% of services sold	Achieve high-tech services sales proportion of 45%	
	System skills	Input all service record changes	Accurate and up-to-date service records	100% accurate statements issued within twelve hours of end of service week	Maintain adequate caregiver pool	
	Product knowledge		Timely customer statements	100% of caregivers paid accurately within five business days of end of service week		
Account Technicians	System skills	Send statements on time	Timely and accurate caregiver payments	95% achievement of monthly sales target		
	Service pricing knowledge	Identify and resolve billing and service record discrepancies		Cases staffed on customer start request		
	Ability to retrieve record data in response to service representative queries	Send timely and accurate payments to caregivers				
	Ability to identify/correct billing invoice					
	Ability to identify/resolve disparities between billing data and service records					
	Knowledge of how system drives business processes					
Shift Supervisors	Ability to use system data for performance improvement	Use system data to identify emerging problems and provide effective coaching	Competent staff performance			
	Ability to provide on system operations	Train new service reps	Timely resolution of performance problems			

work done by the early implementers of the laptop initiative referred to earlier. When the impact model is a final deliverable, then it is important to pay particular attention to its format and structure to be sure it employs the correct terminology that the client will find acceptable. When the impact model is not a final deliverable, it can be less formal, because once it is developed and used for understanding, it can be discarded. We have, for example, created impact models using Post-it notes, index cards, newsprint, chalkboards, and even in some cases, cocktail napkins, and beer glass coasters.

5.

Using a Survey to Search for Best and Worst Cases

This chapter describes the process and tools used to search for and identify the most likely success cases—the stories that you need to understand and tell—to figure out how well a new initiative is working. A new initiative may involve many people—from dozens in a small organization to hundreds and even thousands in a larger organization. Who among all these people is having the most rich and informative experience? Who is having success? Who is not? Whose story should be told? Whose experience will enable the greatest learning so that the initiative can be made more effective and successful?

The *survey* step of the SC inquiry process addresses these questions. We put the word survey in italics, because though this step is very often accomplished with a written survey questionnaire, this is not always the case. Sometimes it is possible to use other methods to accomplish the survey purpose of locating the most likely and informative success cases.

This chapter provides detailed guidance to help readers:

- Plan the best survey method to use
- Design and administer the survey
- Analyze the data to identify potentially best and worst success cases

A High Level Look at the Survey Process

It is easiest to think about where this step begins by first thinking about where it needs to end. What we are looking for in a Success Case study is the right stories to tell—stories of success (or lack of it) that will help us quickly understand how well our program is working, why, and what needs to be done to make it work better. To accomplish this, we need to have a way to sort through all of the potential cases—each and every person involved in the program or change initiative—and figure out what small handful of those is worth following up with an in-depth interview. This "sorting out" is the survey step. By the end of this step, we want to know:

- Who is using the change to the greatest extent?
- Who is not using the change?
- Who is having the greatest success?
- Who is having the least success?
- Who among all of these potential successes and nonsuccesses are the most likely candidates for an interview?

Often, a traditional survey questionnaire, either written or email, is the best route to this end. The advantage of such a survey is that it can provide some further quantitative information about the nature and scope of the success. That is, after a survey, we may be able to conclude that, for instance, "Sixty-three percent of all the sales representatives who were provided a laptop have used it for at least one of the four key applications."

Because a survey is the most common and the most useful and informative method for locating potential success cases, the bulk of this chapter is devoted to success case surveys: what they look like, how they work, and how to create them. But before going into more detail about SC surveys, we will review the alternative (nonsurvey) methods.

Alternatives to the Formal Survey

Table 5.1 presents a list of some of these nonquestionnaire survey methods for identifying potential success cases. The list is not exhaustive, because we create new or revised methods as we need them, depending on the circumstances of the program we are studying. In a study of a new online training process, for example, we were able to use the records of trainees who had accessed and completed the study modules, because these data were already tracked by the system. In this instance, it was a simple matter to locate the few individuals who had completed the training modules, scored the highest on the module quizzes, and logged back on to request assistance in applying the training. There was no need for a survey, as the system data pinpointed the most successful users. Locating nonusers was likewise easy, because we simply drew a random sample from among those employees not on the user list.

The left-hand column in Table 5.1 describes the Success Case identification method. The right-hand column provides a brief example of how we have used the method. Again, readers should note that the list is representative only of some methods used in past SC studies; additional methods are waiting to be invented, limited only by the reader's creativity.

Table 5.1

Some Useful Success Case Identification Methods

Success Case Identification Method	Examples
Analysis of employee performance data or records	In studying the successful use of a new sales technique, we found the branch offices that reported the best sales for the two quarters following the introduction of the technique. Then, by calling each of the highest-sales offices and speaking with the branch manager, we asked for the top three employees.
	In the service department of an automobile dealership, we used repair records to discover who completed repairs in the shortest time with the greatest success (scored by lack of call-backs from customers). These successful repair technicians were then interviewed to find out what diagnostic tools and methods they used.
Analysis of end-user	In a financial services company, we identified the top 3% of service advisors who had earned the highest customer satisfaction ratings. By interviewing these few people, we were able to find out which of the support tools and services they used and to which they attributed their success.
Word of mouth and reputation	In a financial services company, we identified the most successful field office managers by asking the executive team to identify their "star" performers.

Table 5.1 *(continued)*

Some Useful Success Case Identification Methods

Success Case Identification Method	Examples
Word of mouth and reputation *(continued)*	In a school district, we asked school principals which teachers had the greatest reputation among parents for sensitivity and caring.
Analysis of usage records and data	To identify the most successful performers in a call center, we analyzed call data to see who completed the most calls per hour.
	In a high school library, we analyzed checkout records to identify those students who checked out the most curriculum-related materials in the past semester.
The "grapevine"	In a welfare agency, we asked a few managers to tell us who among their staff were the most informed and up-to-date on current office affairs. We then asked these people to tell us who were the two best welfare service workers. We kept asking until no new names arose and chose for our interviews those workers whose names were referenced the most often.

The Formal Success Case Survey

There are two fundamental types of SC surveys. One is the survey with the single intent of identifying the most likely potential success cases. This type of survey is intended only to "sort out" from among all the participants in a program those who report the most, and the least, success with that particular intervention or program. This single-purpose survey can be very brief, because it is not intended to gather information other than the minimum needed to discriminate highly successful and highly unsuccessful users or participants from all of the rest. In a study of the success of an initiative that introduced new software for service technicians, for example, the survey had only four items corresponding to the four possible applications of the software. Each item asked the respondent to check the item if that particular application had been used, then to rate on a five-point scale how successful the application had been (from "very clear success with a measurable outcome" to "no noticeable success at all").

The second type of survey has an extended aim of gathering additional information about the nature and scope of success and may seek further information as well. In a recent SC study for a large automobile producer, for example, we were attempting to gauge the success of a program that provided training and professional assistance to auto dealerships via a dedicated satellite television network. The survey in this example was fairly extensive and had the following parts:

1. Demographic items to describe the role and other characteristics of the respondent
2. Items to report which of the several categories of television services offered respondents had actually used
3. Rating of the success respondents could report based on their usage of each service
4. Reactions about the user-friendliness of the service system
5. General attitudes toward the helpfulness or lack of helpfulness of this and other corporate services

Which type of survey to use depends, of course, on the purpose of the SC study and the scope of the questions it is seeking to answer. We begin our discussion of SC survey methods with the single-purpose survey.

The Single-Purpose Survey

Again, this sort of survey has a limited and narrow function: simply to identify the most and least successful participants in a program from among all of the participants. In essence, this type of survey has only one question to ask: "To what extent have you been able to use [name of the program or service] to achieve success on [name of the overall organization business goal]?"

For the sake of reliability of measurement and to help spread out the respondents so it is easy to identify the top and bottommost among the successes, this type of survey will most likely include a small number of items, typically no more than five to seven or so. Even though there are these five to seven actual items, the central aim of the few items is to answer the question: Who is using it the most and least, and who is having the greatest and least success?

Figure 5.1, by way of example, shows the entire survey for a recent SC study that was intended to explore the success of a program that supplied online tools (job aids, assistance) to procurement managers in a telecommunications company. The survey was conducted via email so there was no need for the survey to include a name or other identifying information (this information was already available from the company's database of employees). We did have to be sure, however, that the survey software and response method (going to a URL address to respond to the survey) would not erase the respondent's name!

Figure 5.1
Procurement Manager Survey

Here is a list of some of the ways that some people have used the XYZ Procurement System Tools. Please rate the extent to which you have been able to apply, or not, your training to each of the applications listed. (Check the appropriate box in each row.)

Application	Tried this and had clear and concrete positive results	Tried this but no clear results yet	Tried this somewhat but don't expect any results	Have not tried this application at all
Used the tools to secure a new and better contract with a new supplier	( )	( )	( )	( )
Used the tools to negotiate a reduced price with a current supplier	( )	( )	( )	( )
Used the tools to secure more favorable supply conditions (e.g., faster delivery)	( )	( )	( )	( )
Used the tools to avoid a cost increase on an existing contract	( )	( )	( )	( )

What to Notice About Figure 5.1

This brief survey shown in Figure 5.1 is a very typical SC survey questionnaire. It is purposely very brief, as a brief survey is more likely to lead to high rates of response (we typically experience 80% or higher response rates in most of our SC studies). Here are some other key features to note about the survey in Figure 5.1.

- The survey is not anonymous. In an SC case study, we have to be able to follow up on those few respondents who we think might represent true success and nonsuccess cases. Thus, we need to link each survey response to an identified individual. In analysis, however, we will promise that all responses will be treated as if they were anonymous (that is, never identifying a success case by name).

- The item "stems" in the left-hand column contain a two-part structure: Each item asks about (1) usage that has (2) led to a worthwhile business result. An SC study always aims to discover who has used some new initiative or program to achieve some sort of result that is known to be of value to the organization.

- The items focus on a few key and specific behavioral applications; the items do not ask about reactions or feelings.

- The scale for response is broad and has sufficiently extreme anchor points at each end of the scales continuum to produce "ceiling." That is, we want the survey to spread respondents out across a sufficiently wide distribution so that only a few end up in the highest, and lowest, response categories. Notice that we would not get sufficient discrimination between groups of respondents were we to ask the question with just two response choices (e.g., "I tried it" and "I did not try it").

Nor would we get sufficient a spread of responses if we made the extreme anchor statements too weak and pallid. The high (successful) end of the scale should be quite rigorously high, and the low (nonsuccessful) end of the scale should be quite rigorously low.

- The survey asks only what it must to discriminate among high and low successes. We do not embellish the survey with "nice to know" items or ask anything we do not absolutely need to, as additional items will hurt response rates.

- We do not ask on the survey what we can find out elsewhere. Notice, for example, we do not ask the respondent to identify his or her job title or number of years with the company. We may wish to know these things for purposes of analysis, but we can get this information elsewhere, that is, from the company's database.

Notice that the survey in Figure 5.1 could be analyzed to provide a quantitative estimate of how many respondents had claimed success with each particular application possibility. That is, we could report, for instance, that: "Eighteen percent of the procurement audience reported usage of the training to achieve a clear and specific cost reduction in an existing contract." Or, another conclusion from the survey might be: "The most common usage of the new tools (33% of respondents) was to secure new contracts, while only 12% of the respondents used the tools to improve procurement conditions for existing contracts." So, even though the survey is brief, and even though success cases will be described in qualitative, narrative language, the survey data can be used to provide reliable estimates of impact and usage.

The content for the items in the survey is based on the impact model (discussed in Chapter Four). The impact model on which the survey in Figure 5.1 is based would have indicated that there were four intended critical behavioral applications of the new tools program and that the business results aimed for were to acquire new and better procurement contracts or to renegotiate existing contracts for better conditions. If, in this example, the applications were not known beforehand, then the survey would have simply asked, with just one or two items, if the respondent had used the new tools *in any way* to achieve *any sort* of valuable result.

The Broader, Multipurpose Survey

As we noted, sometimes the survey is intended to provide a more broad and diverse range of information than simply identifying the highest- and lowest-success participants. For example, we might want to identify which participants were involved as volunteers in the program versus those who were pressured or coerced into participating. Or, we might wish to ask respondents which of several support factors (a supervisor's encouragement, or an incentive, for instance) they experienced that enhanced or inhibited their success.

Figure 5.2 provides an example of a more extensive survey. The example in this case was a study of engineering training (in failure mode effects analysis [FMEA]) provided to engineers and other internal and external design staff in a big-three automobile company.

Figure 5.2
FMEA Evaluation: Participant Survey

Please provide the following information, which will help us assess the value of the FMEA program. All responses will be treated confidentially. Code numbers are used only for analysis purposes; all codes and identification will be destroyed after report completion. Absolutely no participants or specific comments will be individually identified to [the company] or to anyone else.

Part A: Background Information

1. Check the box that describes your employment status when you participated in the FMEA course.

   ☐ Company employee
   ☐ Employee/contractor of company supplier
   ☐ Other noncompany participant
      (Please describe.):_____

2. Which of the following best describes your primary role or responsibility?

   ☐ Product engineer
   ☐ Process engineer
   ☐ Manager
   ☐ Other *(Please describe.)*:_____
   _____

Figure 5.2 *(continued)*
FMEA Evaluation: Participant Survey

3. Prior to participating in the FMEA course, what was your work experience with FMEA? (Please check the best response.)

   ☐ None (I had never participated in an FMEA.)

   ☐ Limited (I had participated in FMEAs perhaps one to three times total.)

   ☐ Moderate (I had participated in FMEAs from time to time, as necessary.)

   ☐ Extensive (I had participated in FMEAs often; they were an integral part of my work processes.)

4. Had you participated in any formal FMEA instruction prior to this course?

   ☐ Yes

   ☐ No

5. What approximate proportion of the other employees in your work group has completed FMEA training?

   ☐ None

   ☐ Less than half

   ☐ About half

   ☐ More than half

   ☐ All

Figure 5.2 *(continued)*
FMEA Evaluation: Participant Survey

For Questions 6 through 10 below, please describe your workplace's environment regarding FMEA by agreeing or disagreeing with each statement below. Enter one of the following numbers beside each item to identify how strongly you agree or disagree with that item.

1 = Strongly disagree
2 = Disagree
3 = Agree
4 = Strongly agree

_____ 6. My work unit has never advocated the use of FMEA.

_____ 7. FMEA is performed only when a supervisor instructs us to.

_____ 8. FMEA is a form that we know we have to complete.

_____ 9. FMEA is considered a valuable tool by my team, but we aren't given the time to do it the way we should.

_____ 10. FMEA is considered an essential tool that is ingrained in our work processes.

_____ 11. Check the *one* response that best represents your personal accountability for FMEA.

☐ My supervisor monitors how well I use FMEA and holds me accountable for resolving critical failure modes and effects.

☐ My supervisor expects me to use FMEA but does not typically follow up on the quality of my FMEAs or their results.

☐ I don't know what my supervisor's expectations are regarding FMEA.

☐ My supervisor does not hold me accountable for applying FMEA.

Figure 5.2 *(continued)*
FMEA Evaluation: Participant Survey

Part B: Your FMEA Course Experience

12. I participated in the FMEA course as a result of:

    ☐ A training planning process initiated by my supervisor

    ☐ A training planning process initiated by myself

    ☐ My assignment to a project mid-year that required FMEA
    Other (Please explain.): _____

    _____

13. I attended FMEA training as:

    ☐ A member of an intact work group or team

    ☐ An individual participant

14. My FMEA training: (Check one.)

    ☐ Was conducted for my team to complete the FMEA for
    a specific project.

    ☐ Was timed to occur right before I needed to actually
    apply FMEA on the job.

    ☐ Was scheduled at my convenience (without regard to
    when I might need to apply FMEA).

15. When you finished the FMEA course, how confident were
    you that you could complete an actual FMEA? (Check one.)

    ☐ I felt very confident that I had the knowledge and skills
    I needed to complete an FMEA.

    ☐ I felt that I had learned some basic knowledge and
    skills about FMEA but was uncertain that I could
    complete an FMEA on the job without additional support.

    ☐ I did not feel that the course gave me the knowledge
    and skills necessary to complete an FMEA.

Figure 5.2 *(continued)*
FMEA Evaluation: Participant Survey

16. Which of the following best represents your understanding of FMEA since the workshop? (Check one.)

    ☐ FMEA is too cumbersome for regular use.

    ☐ FMEA is one of several useful quality tools; others may be more effective.

    ☐ FMEA is a framework for thinking about all of my work.

Part C: FMEA Experience Since Completing the Course

17. Place a checkmark in the box beside any of the following projects that you have been involved in since the FMEA course. (Check all boxes that apply.)

    ☐ I participated in a new design project.

    ☐ I participated in a design change project.

    ☐ I had some other FMEA opportunity. *(Please describe.)*

    _____

    _____

18. How many times would you estimate you've participated in an FMEA since the course?

    ☐ None

    ☐ One

    ☐ To or three

    ☐ More than three

If you've participated in any FMEAs since the course, continue with Item 19.
If you haven't participated in any FMEAs since the course, skip to Item 23.

Figure 5.2 *(continued)*
FMEA Evaluation: Participant Survey

19. What was your role in the FMEA process? (If you've partici-
    pated in more than one FMEA, you may check as many
    boxes as apply.)
    ☐ Acted as team leader
    ☐ Acted as team member
    ☐ Completed the FMEA without a team
    ☐ Guided a supplier through the FMEA process
    ☐ Reviewed a completed supplier FMEA form, but was
       not otherwise involved in the FMEA
    ☐ Other (Please specify.): _____
       _____

20. The FMEA process sometimes includes certain process steps.
    Which of the following steps did your FMEA process
    include? (Check all that apply.)
    ☐ Organize project team
    ☐ Identify scope of project
    ☐ Identify critical failure modes and effects
    ☐ Recommend corrective actions
    ☐ Complete the FMEA form
    ☐ Gain management approval of recommendations
    ☐ Implement and monitor recommendations

21. Please rate the significance of the FMEA process itself as
    you have used it since training. *(Check one.)*
    ☐ FMEA was a requirement that produced no results of value.
    ☐ FMEA revealed data that could have been gathered
       using common sense.

Figure 5.2 *(continued)*
FMEA Evaluation: Participant Survey

☐ FMEA helped us identify some potentially critical failures, but no corrective actions have yet been taken.

☐ FMEA identified potentially critical failures that we would not have otherwise detected until after product release; recommended corrective actions are under way.

22. As you review your FMEA experience, what factors (if any) helped you use FMEA effectively? (Check any that apply.)

☐ My understanding of and skill in the FMEA process and tools

☐ My belief that FMEA is essential to our work

☐ Clear management direction that FMEA is to be taken seriously

☐ Availability of technical support on the job (e.g., application engineering support)

☐ Availability of coaching and support from co-workers experienced in FMEA

☐ Budgeted and planned FMEA time and resources

☐ Work environment in which team work is valued and promoted

☐ Other *(Please describe.)*: _____

_____

23. As you review your FMEA experience, what factors (if any) hindered your ability to use FMEA effectively? (Check any that apply.)

☐ My incomplete understanding of the process

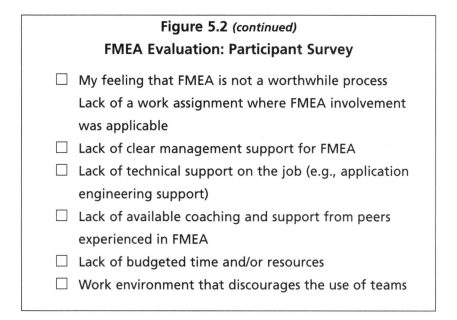

Figure 5.2 *(continued)*
FMEA Evaluation: Participant Survey

☐ My feeling that FMEA is not a worthwhile process

  Lack of a work assignment where FMEA involvement
  was applicable

☐ Lack of clear management support for FMEA

☐ Lack of technical support on the job (e.g., application
  engineering support)

☐ Lack of available coaching and support from peers
  experienced in FMEA

☐ Lack of budgeted time and/or resources

☐ Work environment that discourages the use of teams

What to Notice About the Survey in Figure 5.2

Clearly, the survey shown in Figure 5.2 goes well beyond the more simple and limited-purpose survey shown in Figure 5.1. Indeed, the evaluation for which this longer survey was used approached a more traditional sort of survey-based evaluation, of which a Success Case study was an integral part. In other words, the survey portion of the SC study was intended to produce some meaningful and generalizeable results on its own. The subsequent Success Case analysis then augmented these survey findings and provided richer illustration of the impact of the training program. In reality, we would not have recommended a survey of this length as response rates would probably be too low because most respondents would not take the time needed to complete it. In this case, however, the client was able to assure response through administrative requirements.

Here are some other key features to notice about the survey shown in Figure 5.2.

- The demographic data collected in Part A was not otherwise available because many of the respondents were contractors and other nonemployees. Further, these data were important to analysis, as we needed to differentiate findings according to the demographic status of the participants.

- Items 6 through 10 were used to check the conditions under which participants attended the training, as there was a strong suspicion (based on informal inquiry prior to the study) that much of the program was not having an impact due to its mandatory "forced attendance" policies. Other items also checked for these sorts of attitudes, which might influence impact.

- Part B asked questions about the training experience itself. In this case, the client needed such information. And, as noted previously, we were concerned that the nature of the training experience (e.g., whether it was done alone or with a group) might influence its impact.

- Part C explored what participants had done after the course. These categories of application were derived from the impact model (as explained in Chapter Four) that we created prior to construction of the survey. It was obvious during the information gathering we did to create the impact model that at least some groups of participants would see FMEA as a burdensome but mandatory bureaucratic requirement. Our hunches and suspicions about impact conditions led us to include items such as are found in Part C.

- Items 22 and 23 asked about conditions that might have helped or hindered impact. These sorts of factors are always included during the SC interview portion of the study. In this

case, however, there were several hundred training participants, and we would interview only a very small number.
Thus, we felt the survey portion of the study, which was sent
to a large sample of participants, needed to assess these factors
in order to make meaningful and defensible generalizations
about their impact.

Readers should note again that the sort of survey they need to use—
brief and single purpose or broader—must be decided upon by referring
to the overall purpose for their SC study. The trick is to use a survey that
will reliably collect the data needed to serve the purposes of the study.
Sometimes this will call for a quite limited and brief survey; other times
a more complex survey is required. Only rarely will a survey of the
length and complexity such as that shown in Figure 5.2 be needed.

Survey design and construction is, it should be noted, a relatively
sophisticated skill that requires technical expertise and knowledge. It is
beyond the scope of this book to provide such expertise within these
pages. Readers who do not have a lot of expertise are strongly advised to
get expert help for the construction of surveys, unless it is clear that a
rough "homemade" version will be suitable. Readers would also do well
to refer to some of the many books that have been written about the art
and science of survey construction. One such excellent and exhaustive
resource is Babbie's (1990) book titled *Survey Research Methods*.

Devising a Scoring Scheme

A major consideration in designing the survey instrument is the construction of a scoring scheme. Remember: A major function of the survey is to allow you to select potential success and nonsuccess candidates
from among your survey respondents. Then you will choose and interview these potential success cases (as explained in the next chapter) to
develop your final success case reports, and you will interview nonsuc-

cesses to learn why they were not successful. Thus, you need a way to determine which respondents represent the greatest and least potential successes. Devising a scoring method is relatively easy, but it is important that you do it before finalizing your survey forms. If your survey does not allow easy and sufficient scoring, then it is too late to change it if you have already sent it out.

Figure 5.3 excerpts the questions from a simple SC survey. Following the example survey questions is a discussion of how we constructed a "score" for the survey that was used to rank respondents from the highest to the lowest.

Figure 5.3
Example SC Survey Questions
(to Show Scoring Method)

Survey Questions

1. I have used the development planning tools to take more responsibility for my own performance and development.
   a. Yes, with clearly positive results
   b. Yes, but I haven't experienced any discernible results yet
   c. Not yet, but I expect to
   d. I don't have any plans to do this

2. I have used the development planning tools to foster a more positive relationship with my manager.
   a. Yes, with clearly positive results
   b. Yes, but I haven't experienced and discernible results yet
   c. Not yet, but I expect to
   d. I don't have any plans to do this

Figure 5.3 *(continued)*
Example SC Survey Questions
(to Show Scoring Method)

Survey Questions

3. Which of the following best represents the extent to which you have used the development planning process tools?
   a. I have completed a development plan that has since been put into action with a positive result.
   b. I have completed a plan, but it has not been put into action yet.
   c. I have started a plan, but it isn't complete yet.
   d. I intend to develop a plan, but haven't started yet.
   e. I have no intentions of developing a plan.

4. Which statement best represents your feelings about your manager's commitment to development planning?
   a. I think my manager has a sincere interest and is fully committed to helping employees grow and perform to their fullest ability.
   b. I think my manager means well, but has not committed fully to the effort.
   c. I think my manager sees this process as little more than an administrative requirement.
   d. I think my manager has no commitment at all to this process.

Figure 5.3 *(continued)*
Example SC Survey Questions
(to Show Scoring Method)

5. Which statement best represents your own commitment to development planning?
   a. I have a sincere interest and am fully committed to growing and performing to my fullest ability.
   b. I am mostly positive, but have not committed fully to the effort yet.
   c. I think this process is little more than an administrative requirement.
   d. I have no commitment at all to this process.

To earn the highest possible score, respondents must have answered Questions 1 and 2 with choice (a). That is, they must have reported a clearly positive outcome in each of the two categories. Item 2 was scored with four (4) points for choice (a), 3 for (b), 2 for (c), 1 for (d), and zero for choice (e). Responses to items 3 through 5 were scored (3) points for response choice (a), 2 points for (b), 1 point for (c) and zero points for (d). In this way a total score was calculated so that respondents could be ranked from highest to lowest. Then, it was a simple matter of choosing the few highest scores for an interview, because these were possible success cases. As it turned out, there were very few in the highest category, but a lot of very low scores. This being the case, we also chose some of the very lowest scoring respondents for an interview, as it was helpful to learn why the program seemed to be so unsuccessful for so many people.

Be sure to provide enough "ceiling." As you review your scoring scheme, you need to be sure that you have not made your test for success too easy (or too hard). That is, when you get your responses back, you would not want your survey to have defined success so laxly that virtually all of your respondents claimed great success. Although it is possible that everyone has indeed been successful, experience says that this is not likely. In the rare instances when the program has in fact worked so well that huge numbers have been successful, you need to be sure that this high reporting of success is based on a sufficiently rigorous definition. On the other hand, you do not want to have defined success so rigorously that no one could have possibly achieved it. The key here is to provide enough response choices across a wide range of possible outcome scenarios. This will assure that your survey will produce enough spread in all scores that you have the relatively small extreme groups you will need to explore success cases in depth during the interview process.

A Scoring Glitch (an Early Learning Experience)

My doctoral advisor had graciously made my services available to a consulting firm that had a contract to collect data on high schools with drug problems. Because I was the junior staff member and a lowly graduate student, the evaluation team leaders graciously assigned me to collect data from the poorest and toughest inner city neighborhoods on Philadelphia's north side. To assure comparability of data, all interviewers were using a formal set of questions and had been told to rigorously follow the scoring and rating scheme. Interviews were conducted with small groups of students assembled by cooperating school principals. I met with my first group on the first day of the study—a mixed race band of smirking long-haired, leather-clad, tattooed young men who regarded me with obvious disdain. But I was soon able to create a constructive and open atmosphere, and we proceeded to my being able to ask the first question on the survey, which was: "Do you think there is a drug problem in your school?" The scoring instructions called for me to ask the group to rate the severity of any drug problem from "very bad" to "not a problem at all." Lively discussion ensued, and it was soon clear that my group (and several others later in the day) had a viewpoint considerably different from that envisioned by the survey designers. My group of students talked and argued for a while, then agreed on a rating. Their consensus was to rate the interview item "not a problem at all." Why? It was clear from their discussion that they felt that most students would not have any problem getting pretty much any drug they wanted! If there were any problem, it would be in getting enough money to get the really good stuff, but a little shoplifting or stealing readily solved these money problems, they agreed, and so overall, getting drugs was not a problem! I dutifully returned my interview score data, pointing out the different point of view taken by the inner city respondents. The complete reversal of the intended scoring, of course, invalidated the overall data and made it impossible to interpret.

Planning the Success Case Survey

There are several considerations that must be made in planning the survey process. These include deciding on timing, determining the numbers of people to survey, and creating an administration plan to distribute and recover completed surveys.

How Soon to Survey?

A question that is always asked by new SC Method users is: How long after a program should we follow up participants (e.g., one month? six months? longer)? The determining variable is this: How long after the introduction of a change would you reasonably expect that participants should have had an ample opportunity to use the innovation? Consider, for example, our recent experience in a customer service call center where we were evaluating the introduction of new call distribution software and the training associated with it. In this case, the impact of usage of the new software on customer waiting time and the accuracy of distribution of calls to a qualified service rep should have been almost immediate. The new software was installed and the training had been provided. The launch of the innovative software was scheduled for midnight Monday (the start of the service week). It was clear that, if the training had been effective, service reps should be using the system effectively and that customers should be experiencing reduced call-wait times and improved accuracy within the first few days after the launch. Our follow up was thus conducted the very next week. This tight schedule was also driven by the understanding that the client needed to make revisions to the system very quickly because loss of business would ensue if the new system could not be made to work well, for all call center employees, right away.

In the case of the procurement tools provided to purchasing department agents, however, we decided not to survey the participants until six months after the introduction of the tools. In this case, the pace of work was such that purchasing agents typically negotiated new or revised contracts only once every one to two months. So, to allow the new tools a fair trial period, and to be sure that there was enough opportunity for users to have tried them out on a reasonable range of application scenarios, six months seemed to be the best choice.

Again, the rule here is to determine the duration of time after the introduction of a new program or initiative within which the innovation can reasonably be expected to have worked, if it were going to work at all. This time-lag estimate is then balanced by the urgency of the client's need to know something about successful impact. It may be that the innovation would need fully six months to be completely effective, but the client needs to make a decision sooner than that. If this is true, a shorter delay would be advised. On the other hand, we do not want to let the urgency of the client's need create a demand that is unreasonable. It may be that collection of success data earlier than is reasonable would introduce too much bias and inaccuracy into the results. If this were the case, we would advise our client that although it is possible to get an answer sooner, that answer will be too unreliable to be useful.

How Far Back in Time to Survey?

A related timing issue is the question of how far back in time one delves for success cases. In the case of the emotional intelligence training for financial advisors, for example, the program had been running for more than five years. It was theoretically possible in this instance to include all participants from the past five years in our survey sample. We felt, however, that it would not be wise to do so. The SC Method seeks objective, behavioral, and verifiable accounts of people's usage of new programs and tools. Going back over a five-year duration would have introduced too much unreliability into the data. The frailty of human memory, the pace of turnover of employees, changes in record keeping, and the minor (though cumulative) changes that had been made in the training program over the five-year period all combined to convince us that this was just too long a period of time from which to sample. Further, there were sufficient numbers of employees in the several categories of interest who had completed the training in the past year to give us large enough samples with which to work. Our general "rule of thumb," to protect the integrity and defensibility of the SC data we collect, is that we do not go back farther than nine to twelve months after the stabilization of a change or innovation.

Do You Need to Survey Everyone?

How many participants do we pursue? Do we employ a sample or survey every participant? Clearly, you do not want to spend more time and effort than is necessary to get the information you need to gauge the impact of innovations and changes. On the other hand, you do not want to end up with an SC study that does not give you enough information to draw any reasonable conclusions. Although sampling theory and methods are very powerful tools, they are also the provinces of sophisticated research experts. Fortunately, there are some relatively simple rules we can provide that readers can rely on to guide their practical application of the SC Method. In the unusual instances where more complex sampling will be needed, we advise securing expert assistance.

Almost never will you need to pursue each and every participant in a program, unless the number of participants is very small to begin with. What is "small"? The cut-off point that we apply in typical SC practice is about forty to fifty participants.* If the number of participants is around fifty or so, it is best to survey all of them. If the number is 400 or greater, then a 10% sample will work, because this 10% sample will yield the cut-off number of forty to fifty participants. This assumes, of course, that your response rate is good enough that the sample you actually end up with will be larger than forty to fifty participants. To be safe, we pessimistically assume that we will get only a 50% response rate, thus we double all of our lowest sample-size estimates. In other words, if we have a total of 100 participants, we will just go ahead and survey all of them. We know that we would like to end up with a final number of about fifty actual participants from which to select our most and least successful participants for follow-up interviews.

---

*This number is derived from sampling and probability theory which directs that, with random samples, one needs roughly a 10% sample, or a minimum of thirty-four or so cases from a population in order to make a defensible general estimate of the parameters of a population within known estimates of certainty. The number of forty to fifty is suggested to err on the side of too many, versus too few. Again, for readers seeking further information, the Babbie (1990) text is recommended.

Table 5.2 summarizes these sampling rules into a handy guide.

Table 5.2
A Rough and Ready Sample-Size Guide

Small (100 or less) number of participants	Large (800 or more) number of participants	In-between numbers (100–800) of participants
Survey all participants, to assure that you end up with at least fifty or so responses. Because you have not sampled at all, probability estimates and related sample sizes do not apply.	Choose a minimum 10% random sample. Assuming a worst-case response rate of 50%, you will end up with the requisite forty-plus responses.	Choose a sample of at least 10%, or larger, as needed to produce a sample of at least 80–100, thus assuring (after nonresponses) that you end up with the requisite forty-plus responses.

Subdividing a Population of Participants

In some SC studies, we are investigating the success of a program that has involved different job roles and job settings. In the automobile dealership study, for instance, we felt that the size and nature of the dealership might have been related to the success of the satellite system program. Thus, there were three major categories of dealerships: urban, suburban, and rural. Further, the impact of the program probably differed according to the roles of the participants involved; auto sales reps, service writers, and dealership general managers. When we planned our study, we had to create three versions of the survey—one each for sales reps, service managers, and general managers. Then, we created samples and sample-sizes to correspond to the job roles to which we wanted to draw inferences about program success, within each of the three dealership categories. Because there were large numbers of sales reps, 10% samples would suffice; 10% initial samples yielded ate least 100 sales reps in each of the urban, suburban, and rural categories.

Because there were fewer service writers at each dealership, we drew a thirty sample in each category to give us at least 100 service writers for each type of dealership. Because there was only one general manager at each dealership, we sent a survey to all the general managers.

Note that each category of organizational unit, and each category of job role about which we wish to draw conclusions will drive the decision about sample sizes. Typically, it is best to deal with each subcategory as a different Success Case study (even though they may use essentially the same survey) and apply the general sample-size rules in Table 5.2.

"Reverse Engineering" to a Sample Size

In many SC studies, the simplest way to proceed to figure out how many participants to survey has been to start with the number of final success cases that we wish to create. Sometimes this is limited by the budget available or by the demand for quick information. In one study, for example, the client needed just a couple of success cases to gauge whether a new client intake tool was working. In another study, the budget was such that we knew we could afford to develop only five final success cases. Interviewing Success Case candidates and creating the final success cases is almost always the single most costly study component. Thus, it is sometimes easiest to work backward from this final budget-constrained number to design the initial phases of the study.

Table 5.3 presents a planning framework that can be used to "reverse engineer" the survey and related sample-size plans for an SC study. The example used in Table 5.3 was a study in which the client needed Success Case data for each of three major job roles. The table breaks out each step in our planning/thinking process and provides a handy guide for readers wishing to employ a similar technique.

Table 5.3

A Rough and Ready Guide for Reverse
Engineering Survey Sample Sizes

Step	Example
1. Identify final number of Success Cases needed	We wanted to document a minimum of five final success cases in each of three job role categories.
2. Estimate number of potential success cases necessary to interview in order to arrive at final number needed.	Our experience is that only 50% of potential success cases initially identified will actually result in credible and verifiable success cases that we would be willing to report (roughly one in two will, during the interview, turn out to be "false positives").
3. Estimate the proportion of survey responses that will end up in the highest and lowest potential Success Case category. This is based on how challenging the innovation or program is and how much faith you and your client have that it is (or is not) working successfully.	We typically estimate that "success" will be defined as the highest 15% of all survey respondents. This of course varies with the actual success that a program has achieved. (In one case, we had no success claimed by any survey respondents; in another, success was claimed by more than 70% of the respondents.)
4. Estimate the response rate that you are likely to achieve for your survey (some organizations are notorious for noncompliant employees and vice versa).	Typical response rates for a Success Case survey range from a low of 40% to a high of 90%+ or more. Given that we had high-level authority for our study and a strongly worded cover letter requesting participation in the study, we estimated a response rate of 80%.

Table 5.3 *(continued)*
A Rough and Ready Guide for Reverse Engineering Survey Sample Sizes

Step	Example
5. Do the math. Use your estimates from items 1–4 to figure out how large a sample you will need for your survey.	a. We would need to interview thirty potential success cases to end up with our target of fifteen.
	b. To have thirty potential success cases, we would need to have a final total of 200 survey responses (thirty is 15% of 200; we would select the highest-scoring 15% of all respondents).
	c. If we achieved a response rate of 80%, we would need to initially send out 250 surveys (250 x .80 = 200).

What About Nonrespondents?

Typically, you will not receive a 100% return rate, though we have on rare occasions. Whenever a response rate is relatively low, for instance less than 60%, then one is always confronted with the uncertainty that those who did respond, and those who did not, represent two substantively different groups of people. In other words, you cannot be sure that the information provided by those who did respond can be generalized to those who did not respond. In cases of low response, then, it is wise to temper conclusions and explain the caveat that there may be a response rate bias; that is, that you can't really speak for or about the nonresponse group with any certainty. It may also be wise to try to determine whether there is any response bias at work. This can be done by contacting people in the nonresponse group and asking them questions to ascertain whether it is likely they really differ in any important ways from the group who did respond.

A Final Note on Sampling

This section has dedicated a fair amount of space and attention to the topic of sample size and determination. This should not mislead readers to assume that the SC Method always requires a sophisticated sampling approach. Remember that the principal aim of the Success Case Method is to figure out, quickly and efficiently, which stories of success are most worthy of telling. It may be entirely possible, and often is, to find these success cases without an elaborate or detailed survey process.

There are, however, instances where the SC Method may also be used to extrapolate estimates of how widespread success is or to make statistical inferences about certain groups and their behaviors. If the study needs to culminate in such estimates, for example to determine what proportion of all program participants reported a given level of success or used a certain program element, then some rudimentary use must be made of inferential statistics and sampling. Imagine, for example, that you would like to conclude that "Thirty percent of all participants used their laptops in at least two key sales transactions." In this instance, you must have either (1) provided a survey to all program participants (and have received a high response rate) or (2) drawn an adequately sized random sample from the total population so that you can make estimates within known limits of probable certainty. Again, for readers who will use the SC Method to draw these sorts of conclusions, use of experts and/or reference to professional books is advised.

Creating an Administration Plan

Some Success Case studies will use a written survey reproduced on paper that can be sent or otherwise administered to respondents. More frequently, we rely on email distribution and return of surveys. This electronic survey approach is preferable, as the survey return process also analyzes the data. The software used to create and distribute the survey also automatically keeps a running tabulation of responses and can produce analysis reports on demand. Increasingly, we use email distribution, as it is cheaper, faster, easier for respondents, and it provides instantaneous data analysis.

There are several email and other electronic survey tools available. In many cases, the organization in which the SC study is conducted will already have access to a survey system. There are two primary methods for distributing an email survey. The first is to send the survey itself, by email, to all of the potential respondents. The survey is usually an attachment to a message and can be opened and responded to at the leisure of the respondent. When completed, the email survey is returned (by reply email) to the evaluation team. The second method is to house the survey instrument at a central electronic site (e.g., a Web address). Then, you send a message to the potential respondents to solicit their participation and provide a "hot link" to the survey address. Again, at their leisure, the respondents can link to the survey address and complete the survey. When they are done, the survey is automatically filed. Either method works very well. When using these methods, however, be sure to check that the respondents' names will be retained to identify their individual survey response! Some methods will automatically erase the respondent's name, and thus you are unable to follow up with a Success Case interview. When using an electronic method, get some expert technical advice unless you are a savvy information systems expert.

Whichever method you use, email, paper, or Web survey, it is always a good practice to distribute a letter to all potential respondents to explain the study purposes and solicit their cooperation. This letter should preferably come from a persuasive authority (e.g., the CEO), and it should also assure respondents of confidential treatment.

After your survey is designed, you have determined whether and what samples you will survey, you have a reasonable scoring system, and you have designed a practical distribution and return method, send it out. When your responses come back, you are ready to move to the next to last SC step: selecting Success Case candidates and interviewing them to document your completed Success Case stories.

6.

Interviewing and Documenting Success Cases

This chapter deals with the heart of the SC Method: finding out what stories there are to be told and getting them told in a valid and credible way. The search for success and nonsuccess cases begins with an analysis of the survey data, proceeds with an interview of the potential success cases, and culminates in the documentation of the most poignant and informative stories. Remember that you are looking for a few stories to tell—those few that will best help you and others learn about how well a program or change is working and how you can make it work better. Because you can tell only a few stories, you want to be sure that these few are the absolute best to illustrate and explain success—or the lack of it. You need to document these stories objectively and completely so that they will not lose their persuasive power because they are not credible or cannot be defended as accurate and truthful.

The steps in completing your success case stories are as follows:

1. Analyze the survey responses to identify potential success.
2. Preparing for the interviews.
3. Conduct your SC interviews.
4. Document the most interesting and noteworthy stories.

The following pages of this chapter expand on and illustrate each of these steps. The final section of the chapter includes several Success Case stories drawn from actual SC studies we have conducted. These will serve to illustrate the format of an SC story and will help readers think through their interview preparation so that they will gather enough of the right information to produce stories like these.

Step 1: Analyze the Survey Responses to Identify Potential Success Cases

How you proceed with this step will depend on the purpose of your SC study. You may have a limited purpose study where simple illustration of a few high successes is all that is needed. Or you may have a more complex study purpose. If, for example, you wish to make estimates and conclusions about how widespread certain practices and success results are among certain subgroups of participants, then you will need to think through how to define and select success from among a sub-divided set of survey responses. Or a purpose may be to explore and identify reasons and barriers that kept nonsuccessful participants from achieving the success of others. In these instances, you need to select both highly successful and highly nonsuccessful candidates.

In the more limited purpose study, you are aiming only to capture and document the few most poignant and informative stories. In this limited purpose instance, the identification of success cases is very quick and easy. You simply array your survey responses from high to low and "cream off" the topmost scoring respondents.

If you had 100 respondents, for example, and wanted to develop a final number of three success cases, then you would "cream off" the top six scores—those six surveys that reported the highest usage or success. If there were "ties," that is you had twenty scores that were all the highest, then you would simply pick, at random, just six of these to follow up with an interview.

Why select twice as many candidates as you need? Recall that we estimate that only one out of every two possible successes will actually result in a reportable success story—therefore, if you want to document three final stories, you are advised to choose six possible candidates. If you found that less than three of these initial six turned out to be valid success cases worthy of documentation, not to worry; you just return to your survey results and choose a few more of the highest-scoring respondents.

When your study is broader in purpose, for example to describe factors that inhibit or support success or to draw inferences about the scope of success among participants in different subgroups, then you need a more elaborate selection method. The selection methods for both simple and more complex study purposes are described in the following section.

Choosing the Cases for Interviews

There are several methods you might apply to determine who among the survey respondents to select for an interview. As would be expected, the approach you use to identify interview candidates is determined by the overall purpose for your study.

Table 6.1 provides a listing of the methods we have commonly used to select interview candidates and provides an explanation for each regarding how that method addresses a particular study purpose.

Table 6.1

Methods for Using Survey Scores to Select Success Case Candidates

Study Purpose/Intent	Success Case Selection Approach
You need to capture and document a few of the most dramatic success cases that illustrate the "best" that the program is achieving	Select just a few of the highest scores
You want to illustrate the impact of the program and also to explore factors that seem to support and inhibit success	Select a sample of the highest and lowest scores
You want to illustrate and/or analyze impact in each of several different categories	Select high (and possibly low) scores in each of several categories (different job roles, different organizational units, different types of impact)
You need to not only illustrate impact but also to report the numbers or proportion of participants who used the program successfully. (When you randomly sample from among potential success candidates, you can legitimately draw inferences to the larger group of high-scoring candidates.)	Set a "cut-off" score that defines success; then, randomly sample from among all those respondents who achieved above this score level
You need to report the proportion of success (as above) and also want to report proportions of participants who did not achieve results or receive benefits. This selection framework also lets you compare factors between the extreme groups that seemed to support or inhibit success.	Set a "cut-off" score as above for both the highest level of success and the lowest level of success. Then, randomly sample interview candidates from the highest and lowest extreme groups

Step 2: Preparing for the Interviews

Once you have decided which people you are going to interview as potential success cases, you need to prepare an interview protocol and a general plan for proceeding. Table 6.2 presents some of the usual planning elements that should be considered.

Table 6.2
Some Key Interview Planning Elements

Planning	Element Notes
How many interviewers will you use?	The advantage of using just one interviewer is that you gain the highest amount of reliability in the interview process. With more than one interviewer, there is a chance that each interviewer will conduct interviews differently, thereby biasing the data. Using one interviewer, Although more reliable, may be too much workload for one person. The general rule here is: Use the lowest amount of interviewers possible to get the most reliability and consistency among interviews.
How will you train interviewers?	Interviewing takes practice and expertise. The more interviewers you use, the more elaborate your training must be. Employ sufficient practice. Use two interviewers in early interviews (as a team) so that they can provide one another with feedback. "Eavesdrop" on new interviewers and give them feedback.

Table 6.2

Some Key Interview Planning Elements *(continued)*

Planning	Element Notes
Will you use telephone or face-to-face interviews?	Telephone interviews are usually preferred, because they are far easier to schedule and are typically more convenient for interviewees. Experience shows that telephone interviews are equally productive and accurate when compared to face-to-face interviewing. And, telephone interviewing is also far more economical.
How long should you schedule for each interview?	Most SC interviews can be completed in thirty to forty-five minutes. Best practice is to schedule a forty-five-minute call. If more time is needed, most interviewees will go ahead on the spot and extend the call; if necessary you can call them back later. If the call ends earlier (and many do), the interviewee will probably be grateful for the extra "gift" of unscheduled time.
How many interviews can be conducted in the same day?	Experience says to allow two hours for each interview, at a minimum. This allows time to get ready (and especially to review the interviewee's survey responses, which should be on hand), time for a late start, time for redialing or rescheduling a "no show," and time to review the interview and organize and rewrite notes. The value of extra time to organize notes is vital; you are likely to lose information and confuse data if you plan interviews too close together without a sufficient "cushion" between time to get ready, conduct the interview, and organize notes afterward.

Table 6.2

Some Key Interview Planning Elements *(continued)*

Planning	Element Notes
How will you solicit interviewees' cooperation?	It is common practice to send a communication to the interviewees you select soliciting their agreement to an interview. This can be done with a letter, an email, or a phone call. It is often a good idea to have the communication come from a leader in the organization, as this is more likely to elicit an agreement. This communication should stress the absolutely confidential nature of the interview and that it is to be used only to make judgments about how well a program is working. We commonly ask for agreement, then provide a means (e.g., a reply email) for interviewees to tell us when is the best time to call them for the actual interview.
How will you help interviewees get ready for the interview?	It is often a good idea to send each selected interviewee a reminder notice about their upcoming call and give them a brief preview about what you will want to ask them about. A sentence (or two at the most) is adequate, for example: "During our call, I will be asking you about your experience with _____ program."
Should you tape-record interviews?	Tape-recording is probably not necessary and may inhibit the interviewee's responses. Practiced note-taking is superior to relying on a tape, and experience shows, is highly effective.

The Interview Protocol

Once you have completed your general plan, you are ready to prepare your interview protocol—the form you will use to guide the interview process and remind you of the questions you will ask. The complexity, structure, and detail of the interview protocol will depend on several factors:

- *The skill and experience level of the interviewers:* In general, the more expert and experienced your interviewers are, the less detailed and structured a protocol you will need. In some SC studies where we have relied on just a few highly seasoned interviewers, we have simply provided a brief list of the categories that should be asked about, leaving the exact questions and flow of the interview up to the person conducting the interview. In other cases, where we have had to rely on a larger number of interviewers, we have created a more structured and detailed form for them to follow. In general, however, we have found that it is best to use as little structure as possible, encouraging interviewers to conduct a natural conversation whose flow is dictated by the conversational style and direction of the interviewee.

- *The complexity of data the interview is intended to collect:* In some studies, the Success Case interview is aimed only at understanding and illustrating the nature of usage of a new tool or change. In other studies, the interview is intended to more carefully document usage and identify the more complex nature of factors in the environment that have helped or hindered the interviewee. When the interview is intended to gather a relatively large amount of detailed information, then a more detailed and structured protocol will be needed.

- *The number of interviewers to be involved:* If only one, or a very few, interviewers are to be used in the study, it is less likely that a highly structured protocol will be needed. On the other hand, a high number of interviewers raises the likelihood of unreliability and inconsistency among interviews, in which case a more structured protocol will help to gain more consistency across the many interviews to be conducted.

- *The complexity or uniqueness of the intervention or program that is being studied:* Some SC studies are conducted to assess the impact of very relatively simple innovations and/or programs or interventions with which we, the study directors, are already very familiar. In these cases, we can rely on our experience rather than a highly structured protocol to guide us surefootedly through the interview. On the other hand, the program we are studying may be very complex, with many permutations and variables or be unfamiliar or both! In these sorts of instances, a more structure protocol will be needed to remind the interviewer of questions to ask and to include references to the many parts and nuances of the program being studied.

Filling Buckets: The Protocol Conceptual Model

At the most fundamental level, it is useful to imagine the interview process as a "bucket filling" process. In this imaginary conceit, the interview process aims to fill several information buckets, each bucket representing a certain category of Success Case information. We use a slightly different set of "buckets" depending on whether we are conducting a success interview or a nonsuccess interview.

First, we look at the interview protocol for interviewing Success Case candidates. Figure 6.1 portrays the entire Success Case interview framework as five information buckets. Overall, the interviewer needs to ask questions and guide the conversation to "fill" each bucket with sufficient information about that category. When each bucket is sufficiently filled, the interview is complete.

Figure 6.1
Success Case Interview Buckets

Each information bucket is a general information category. Within each of the five categories ("buckets"), more specific information is as follows:

Bucket 1: **What did they use that worked?**

This category is meant to include the "what, when, how, and where" questions. How did they apply the innovation being studied in the SC inquiry? With whom did they use it? When? Under what conditions or circumstances? What parts of the innovation or training were used the most, least, or not at all? What evidence is there that they really did what they say they did?

Bucket 2: **What results were achieved?**

What outcome(s) did their use of the innovation help achieve? What is different now? What measurable difference was achieved? How do they know they made a difference (e.g., who noticed, what feedback did they get, what changed)? What evidence is there that they really achieved what they say they did?

Bucket 3: What good did it do?

What value was achieved or contributed to? Why are these results important? What business goals were contributed to? What accomplishments were helped or what goals were contributed to? What costs or negative outcomes were avoided as a result of their actions?

Bucket 4: What helped?

What in their environment did they use or access that helped them? Were there any special incentives, rewards, job objectives, work requirements, or so forth that contributed to their success? What about their manager's support (or lack of it) helped or hindered? What tools, references, information sources, or job aids did they use? What seemed to differentiate them from others who did not make such successful use? What about priorities, urgencies, or other extenuating circumstances spurred them to success?

Bucket 5 (optional): Suggestions?

What suggestions (additional program resources, better tools, better incentives, more training, etc.) does the interviewee have that would have increased success? What suggestions can the interviewer make for improvement (these may be based on intuition, hunches, cross-interview observations, etc.)?

With experienced and relatively expert interviewers, it may not be necessary to build an interview protocol any more detailed and structured than the "buckets" graphic in Figure 6.1. That is, the interviewer simply uses the buckets (information categories) as a general guide, then conducts the interview taking notes to "fill" each bucket. The interviewer uses spontaneous probe questions to steer the interview from bucket to bucket as needed. When sufficient information has been gleaned to fill each information category bucket, the interviewer closes the interview. Following the interview, the interviewer writes up the interview, fleshing out the notes taken during the interview itself.

In many SC studies, we have used the "bucket" protocol as our sole interview guide. In these instances, we have found it useful to use a multipage note-taking form, placing a graphic of the information buckets on the front page. Then, stapled to this page are five blank pages, each labeled at the top with its bucket category, one information bucket per page. As the interview progresses, we simply flip from page to page to make the appropriate notes. Often, we will make note of special probe questions that we derive from the interviewee's survey responses. We might ask, for instance: "I notice that you mentioned you used your laptop in a special meeting with your district manager. Can you tell me more about that?"

The principal advantage of this simple interview protocol is its flexibility. Using the bucket structure, we can allow the interviewees to start where they are most comfortable, allowing the conversation to be more natural and spontaneous. An interviewee might, for instance, begin to talk about a barrier saying, for example, "I really scored a win with that new laptop machine." The interviewer would simply begin making notes on the "What good did it do?" bucket-page, then gently steer the conversation from there to other information categories.

The Nonsuccess Protocol

Using the same bucket structure, we can also create a protocol for the instance where we are interviewing people who were especially nonsuccessful. In these cases, the interview structure is even simpler. Figure 6.2 shows the bucket structure for this special nonsuccess interview.

Figure 6.2
Nonsuccess Interview Buckets

Notice that this nonsuccess protocol has only two buckets. The first bucket is labeled "Barriers?" The second bucket is labeled "Suggestions?". Because this interview is conducted with persons whose survey results reported virtually no success at all with the innovation under study, the buckets asking about what was used and what success resulted are not included. In this more focused and brief interview, your principal challenge is to find out what went wrong; what got in the way of using the innovation, and why it was not workable. There are usually two categories of nonsuccess:

- People who didn't even try, for one reason or another, any of the new tools, methods, or learning
- People who tried the new tools or methods, but for some reason did not experience any valuable results

Which category of nonsuccess you are dealing with will be evident from the interviewee's survey responses, so you can proceed accordingly in your interview.

Conducting the nonsuccess interview requires some special sensitivity, in that we don't want to make the person being interviewed feel defensive. We usually start this interview with a sentence or two to this effect: "Our survey showed that several people just were not able, for one reason or another, to do anything much with this [name of initiative] program. As a person who didn't get much value from this effort, what can you tell me about what went wrong? Why didn't this seem to work for you?" As the graphic in Figure 6.2 shows, the nonsuccess interview seeks simply to learn about what factors impeded success and (optionally) what suggestions can be made that would have helped create a more successful experience.

Using a More Elaborate Protocol

As was noted earlier in this chapter, it is sometimes necessary to use a more detailed and structured protocol, as may be the case when using inexperienced interviewers or when the program under study is more complex and difficult to understand. Figure 6.3 provides an example, drawn from a recent SC study, of a more elaborate interview protocol. In this case, there were a number of program factors to be explored, and we were also using nearly one dozen interviewers, thus presenting potential problems with lack of consistency across interviews. The setting is a major automobile company (called here Morton Motors), and the evaluation is focused on the impact of a satellite television provided performance support program called "MortonStar."

Figure 6.3 ELABORATE INTERVIEW PROTOCOL

MORTON MOTOR COMPANY EVALUATION: INTERVIEW PROTOCOLS

Overview

This document contains:

- Detailed outlines of the interview questions that we will ask our Success Case candidates. Once protocol is provided, there are two categories of "success" you may be exploring:

  - Category 1: claimed significant usage and impact

  - Category 2: claimed lesser usage, but some significant impact

- Structure of the protocols

Figure 6.3 ELABORATE INTERVIEW PROTOCOL

MORTON MOTOR COMPANY EVALUATION: INTERVIEW PROTOCOLS *(continued)*

- Each interview protocol has three main components:
  - "Overall questions we are aiming to answer"—use these to help you remain focused on the interview's goal
  - Five numbered "core questions," which are the "big buckets" of information you're seeking. **(The text of each of these questions is printed in bold type.)**
  - Additional "probes," located beneath each core question—use these probes:
    - To help you ask a question in different ways
    - As a "checklist" to ensure you've explored in detail all key aspects of the related core question

NOTE: Probes in bold type are mandatory.

Instructions
To use the protocols effectively, follow these steps:
Review the protocol before an interview, so you're confident of what you need to ask.
Generally, follow the protocol during the interview.
You may ask the questions and probes verbatim as necessary—this is especially helpful to new interviewers.

Remember that Success Case interviews tend not to be linear; that is, you may ask Question 1 and the answer may include information related to Question 3. In this case, code your notes to show where the Question 3 response begins and pursue the Question 3 discussion to its end. You can then jump back to Question 1.

1. *Drill down, drill down, drill down!* Our goal is to get as detailed information as possible on specific examples of successful application of support tools, as well as detailed information on organizational variables that supported or impeded impact.

2. Take detailed, accurate notes during the interview and organize them afterward. Remember to turn your original notes in to the project coordinator with the cleaned up version.

Figure 6.3 ELABORATE INTERVIEW PROTOCOL

MORTON MOTOR COMPANY EVALUATION: INTERVIEW PROTOCOLS *(continued)*

Protocol

Category 1 participants applied learning to a substantial extent and claimed considerable impact. Category 2 participants applied learning to a lesser extent and claimed a more focused positive impact.

Note: In the case of Category 2 participants, adjust the language of each question to reflect a "lower success" level of impact.

Overall questions we are aiming to answer:

- What worthwhile benefits and results did the learner achieve as a result of the performance support? (How well did it work? in detail, with illustrations)
- What factors contributed to the impact?

Core Questions

1. Success of application of learning after engaging in the process

From your survey responses, it looks like you've used your learning from this program effectively and have achieved some pretty good results. I'd like to understand in more detail how you applied your learning and what positive things have happened because of and since the training.

NOTE: Push as far as possible to understand transfer of learning and organizational impact (e.g., more effective performance, increased sales, customer satisfaction improved, work environment more supportive).

Probes:

- How have you used any of the tools provided by the program? (Give a specific example.)
- And then what? And then . . . And what did that lead to?
- How did that help you? What did it achieve?
- What strikes you as the most important benefit you got from applying the tools?
- What benefits to your employer have resulted? (e.g., better employee retention, improved customer satisfaction ratings)
- Give me a specific example of benefits, if you can.

Figure 6.3 ELABORATE INTERVIEW PROTOCOL

MORTON MOTOR COMPANY EVALUATION: INTERVIEW PROTOCOLS *(continued)*

2. Performance system factors that supported the application of learning

How is it that this support seemed to work so well for you, especially since we didn't find this kind of outcome for everyone? As you think about your organization and work environment, what made this work for you?

Probes:

- Your work environment (e.g., office attitude, experience with these sorts of tools)
- Timing of the program?
- Performance measures/expectations?
- Incentives or rewards?
- Experienced peers or support personnel available to help you use what you learned?
- Your personal attitude?
- What are some other motivators that worked for you?

3. Supervisor's role in supporting successful application

One of the things we know sometimes makes a lot of difference is the support of a supervisor.

To what extent is this the case with you?
[IF POSITIVE]
What about your supervisor do you think has helped create a positive result for you? For others?

Probes:
What exactly does your supervisor do that sets him or her apart from others and makes him or her unique? Give me examples, please.
What steps, if any, did your supervisor take to help you prepare for the program and then use what you learned? (e.g., goal setting, providing application opportunities, providing budget and time)
How the respondent got involved in the program

People participate for many reasons. Why/how did *you* get involved in this program?

Figure 6.3 ELABORATE INTERVIEW PROTOCOL

MORTON MOTOR COMPANY EVALUATION: INTERVIEW PROTOCOLS *(continued)*

Probes:

- Who decided you should participate?
- What was the major reason for your attendance?
- What had you heard about the program before participating that influenced your decision?
- Who from your organization was involved in the program (e.g., just self, intact team)?
- What incentives, if any, did you receive for participating?

4. Characteristics of the program itself that made a difference

It sounds like this program had some good outcomes for you. What about the experience itself made it especially successful for you? (Push for detail and examples.)

Probes:

- Concepts and tools presented?
- Design? (Opportunities to apply or practice? Did you get helpful feedback?)
- Delivery? (Facilitator?)
- **MortonStar technology? (strengths and improvements)**
- Timing of the program?
- Other

In this case, the client wanted information about the design of the program, especially the use of the new video format that either helped or hindered success. There were a number of variables we wished to study, and the survey portion of this study had also been relatively complex and detailed. Given these factors, and the fact that we were using a number of interviewers, this more elaborate and structured protocol was needed.

Basic Interview Process

Regardless of the protocol being used, every SC interview follows a basic common structure. Although the "flow" of the interview will be dictated in part by the individual whims of the interviewee and interviewer, the basic structure always reflects the same general sequence.

1. *Opening*: Establish who you are and why you are calling. At this point in the interview, the interviewer makes sure that the person being interviewed understands what the purpose of the call is and that all information is to be treated as anonymous and confidential. Even though you will have sent the interviewee some sort of notice (e.g., an email message) about the purpose of the call and other details, it is always a good idea to confirm that the interviewee is comfortable with the process and has no questions or concerns that may hinder open and frank responses.

2. *Qualification*: Make sure this is really a worthy success case. Not all potential success cases turn out to be valid or confirmable. That is, the interviewee may not have responded accurately or honestly to the survey, thus you have a "false positive" success case. Or, it may be that the success they have claimed is not closely enough linked to a business goal of interest or value or that their results are too vague or are not able to be documented. Thus, the first thing you begin to explore after the opening is the nature of the success the interviewee has claimed, then quickly probe to see if it is worth pursuing further. If it is not, you must graciously close the interview (pretending that you have already gotten all the information you intended to obtain) and thank the interviewee for his or her time. If the success appears to be a valid case, then proceed.

3. *Probing phase:* Get all the information you need to "fill the buckets." This is the major portion of the interview during which you ask enough probing questions to document the success case as well as any helping or hindering factors. During this portion of the interview, it is good practice to occasionally review and summarize what you have learned so far. This gives you time to catch up on your notes, lets you check for accuracy and correct any errors, and also is an excellent time to "shift gears" to steer the interview to a new bucket.

4. *Closing:* Bring the interview to a close and set the stage for any follow-up work you need to do. Most often, when you complete the interview, you are done with the data gathering process. In this instance, thank the interviewee and close the call. At this point, we ask if there is anything else the interviewee would like to tell us or thinks we need to know. We also often provide a telephone number or email address where the interviewee can contact us if there is something else to add. But sometimes there is more information to collect, such as a follow-up call with a third party to confirm an outcome or a reminder to mail a copy of a key document. If the success case appears to be poignant enough that you are sure it is "publishable" (in your final report), you may need to arrange to gather any supporting documentation or confirmation with corroborating sources. Do this before you end your interview. In these instances where there is follow-up work to be done, you may want to ask permission to get back in touch ("May I call you again if I have a question?") should the need arise.

The Two Basic "Steering" Probes

We use two fundamental probe questions to steer an interview in the direction we need it to go. If you are getting a lot of detail about what someone did (how, when, with what steps, and so forth) but you aren't especially clear as to what the value of his or her action is, ask "Why is this important?". This question forces an interviewee to move to the right-hand portion of the impact model—results, business impact. If we have an interviewee who is talking about a lot of outcomes and results, but we're not clear what he or she actually did with the innovation and how he or she used it, we ask, "How did you do that?". The "why" question moves you to hear about impact; the "how" question forces more detail about actions and behaviors.

Documenting Success Cases

The interview process ends with formalizing and documenting the success cases you decide to include in your final report. This may be all of the true success cases you find, or it may be just a selected few that best illustrate and "tell the story" of the innovation you are studying.

Probably the best way to discuss Success Case documentation is to provide an example of a Success Case "story." Figure 6.4 contains an example of an actual success case "impact profile" (our name for a Success Case story). This example comes from the MortonStar program in the automobile company referred to in an earlier example that provided training and technical resources (e.g., compact discs, electronic job aids) to its dealerships. The success story in the example related the impact of some of these resources on the service department of a dealership.

Figure 6.4 Impact Profile: Success Story
at a Morton Motors Auto Dealership

Impact Profile 4—Service Advisor

Impact on Customer Retention

This impact scenario describes a success case in which a new service advisor applied tools and techniques learned in the two *Customers* courses to bring dissatisfied service customers back to the dealership.

Impact at a Glance

Immediate Outcomes
- Three customers who had withdrawn their cars from the dealership's service department returned for continued service.

Business Impact
- Happy customers who keep coming back for vehicles and service (improved CSI scores)
- Increased revenues
- More efficient service operations

The Impact Story

Within the past month, this participant had moved from service cashier to service advisor. One of the first challenges she faced in her new role was dealing with the "mess" left by a service advisor who had just quit the dealership. The former advisor had not effectively handled service requests, with the result that three customers became so dissatisfied that they removed their vehicles from the dealership's service center before service had been performed. (In one case, the dealership had had the car for more than a month with no work performed!)

The new service advisor called all three customers to win back their business. She applied tactics for overcoming negative customer emotions from the *Addressing Concerns* compact disc to defuse the customers' anger. She also applied active listening tactics (e.g., refraining from interjecting before the customers finished speaking) from the *Effective Communication* compact disc. She told the customers that there had been changes made in the service department to address the issues they had faced and asked them to give the dealership another chance. (These were also tactics she learned from the compact disc resources.) In one case, getting the customer back required providing a loaner vehicle for the length of time the customer's vehicle was in service.

Figure 6.4 Impact Profile: Success Story at a Morton Motors Auto Dealership *(continued)*

Immediate Outcomes

By applying key behaviors from these performance resources, the service advisor convinced all three extremely dissatisfied customers to continue to do business with this dealership. All three customers had already removed their vehicles and their business, so, in fact, the ability to address their concerns and effectively communicate reversed a customer satisfaction disaster.

Organizational Impact

Assuming the dealership continues to follow through on the assurances made to these customers, the dealership may have many years of vehicle and service revenues from these customers. In addition, happy customers are much less likely to warn other current customers and more likely to refer new customers to the dealership.

On another note, the service advisor in this case indicates that improved listening skills enabled her to get more information from customers, and thus understand and resolve their needs and concerns more quickly. The advisor is spending less time "fighting fires," because she listens effectively the first time—which allows her more time for proactive, value-added activities on her part. The end result of these changes is both more-efficient performance of the service advisor role and of the service department as well as increased customer satisfaction. The advisor stated that CSI* scores had risen 4.6% from the time she started her new role and she fully expected them to continue to improve.

(Note: CSI scores are based on the company's mandatory customer service satisfaction index as reported by all dealers nationwide.)

What Helped and What Did Not
Contributors:
- Key elements from the two compact discs:
  - Defusing negative customer emotions
  - Listening effectively to a customer's needs and concerns
  - Asking for another chance and making dissatisfied customers whole

- Effective (video-taped) instructors who:
  - Were described by the advisor as knowledgeable and "good"

**Figure 6.4 Impact Profile: Success Story
at a Morton Motors Auto Dealership** *(continued)*

- Kept participant attention, interjected humor, effectively answered questions from the recorded audience
- Workbooks that effectively complemented the compact discs
- MortonStar TV technology that consistently functions properly
- Dealership environment in which:
  - Supervisors suggest training to employees, but only require training that they feel will be valuable for an individual
  - Participants are encouraged to meet after training with their supervisor participating to discuss what they learned, its applications to their jobs, and any questions that remained
- Service manager who provides ongoing coaching to help employees resolve especially difficult customer issues

Barriers:
- First discs received were incompatible format with dealer's equipment; needed to wait three weeks for proper equipment software.

Review Figure 6.4 and notice that the bulk of the Impact Profile is the impact story, which is a summary narration of the success case. This story is just that—a brief story that describes the setting, circumstances, the "action" (what the success case participant did to use the innovation), and the outcomes achieved. The story is factual and includes references to actual facts and data (the rise in CSI scores, for instance).

Notice also that the Impact Profile follows a standard format, as follows:

- Title and identifying information
- "Impact at a Glance" (a brief summary of the overall impact
- Immediate outcomes (the documented basic results or outcomes of the usage of the innovation)

- Business impact—the business goals and/or business value of the immediate outcomes
- The Impact Story
  - Background and setting
  - Immediate outcomes
  - Organizational impact
  - What helped and what did not
    - Contributors
    - Barriers

This format is quite typical of the SC studies we have completed and was arrived at through experience, by trying out various formats and media. Readers are encouraged to innovate and try their own formats and styles for the telling of success case stories. Whatever formats are used, however, should adhere to and enable the application of SC study principles of straightforward storytelling, factual references, and a plain narrative line and style.

Figure 6.5 presents another Success Case Impact Profile. The setting in this instance is a field office for an international development and adoption agency in rural Zimbabwe, Africa. As you will see, this Impact Profile uses names of people (fictionalized) to add dramatic value. The Impact Profile also refers to actual dollar figures to illustrate the business value of the management development program. In this case, the agency had spent considerable resources providing technical assistance to indigenous field office managers. One of the program goals was to promote native persons into positions of leadership and provide them resources to be successful. At the same time, however, a "hard line" faction of the agency's international governing board had insisted that the support program had to "pay its own way." They wanted to see hard evidence that demonstrated the economic value, if any, of the program.

Figure 6.5 Example of Impact Profile with Economic Value of Impact Documented

Impact Scenario 1—Eva Ibay, Operations Manager, Highland Village (Zimbabwe) Field Office

Eva participated in the technical assistance review meeting in the capital city in November 1997 with three professional staff members in the operations department of her field office.

The impact findings are:

Impact at a glance

- Backlog was reduced

- New enrollments were increased

- Office procedures were improved

- Return on training investment to date:

  - For entire office—$82,700

  - Per trainee—$20,675

The Impact Story

During the meeting Eva and her staff talked over dinner about their plans for applying the "Leading at ABC" assistance program and reviewed especially the teambuilding performance tools they had received. They agreed that reducing communication backlogs was their biggest problem. They were receiving low audit scores each quarter, and constant communication pressure was taking time away from working on new enrollment work. Three weeks after receiving the technical assistance package, Eva had a group meeting with her professional staff and they discussed the issues they faced in reducing backlogs. They realized that the three support staff members they worked with could probably play a larger role in organizing communications and decided to meet with them to engage them in some joint problem-solving. At this session, the support staff agreed that there was more they could do and were anxious to play a larger role.

What They Used

First, Eva and the professionals used the "Diagnosing Development Level" process in a group meeting with the support staff and reached agreement on styles and situation. At their "Partnering Performance Meeting," she and the three professional staff members agreed on

Figure 6.5 Example of Impact Profile with Economic Value of Impact Documented *(continued)*

specific performance objectives for operations tasks and results as well as the leadership styles most appropriate for Eva.

Eva next engaged in a "Diagnosis Development" session with the three professionals. Action plans were laid out after this session, and they agreed to monitor results monthly for the next quarter.

What They Achieved

After three weeks, the support staff had designed a new communications planning and monitoring system using the Lotus Notes software the office recently acquired. They also designed and implemented a template for sponsor letters that greatly reduced letter preparation time (previously, all letters were handdrafted individually, then typed). Using the new system, support staff drafted letters that were then reviewed by professionals, who made revisions, then signed off for final production.

Impact

Sponsor communications backlog has been reduced 36%, and for the first time in six years, the recent audit showed the last quarter communications were fully up-to-date (thirty sponsors were removed from the backlog report).

Eva and her staff have been able to spend an average of eight more hours per week on new enrollment initiatives.

New enrollments are 12% ahead of projections this last quarter; twenty-six new enrollments were completed for the period ending March 1, equaling last year's semi-annual production.

Value

According to headquarter estimates, an individual sponsor delay of one quarter reduces responsorship by 22%. Costs of obtaining a new sponsor are $2,600 versus $250 for retaining a sponsor, a difference of $2,350. Using this data, the value of the Highland office's backlog reduction is $70,500 (30 x $2350).

Data on the value of new enrollees is not available from headquarters but is estimated at $2,600, assuming that an applicant sponsor who is denied sponsorship because of lack of enrollees must be replaced by another applicant sponsor. Field office records show staff time per

---

**Figure 6.5 Example of Impact Profile with Economic
Value of Impact Documented** *(continued)*

enrollee is 3.5 hours. Using this estimate, and a total of thirty-two
more hours invested per week by Eva and her three professional staff,
nine of the new enrollees can be attributed to the time freed by the
innovations implemented as a result of the assistance. The value of
this improvement is $23,400 (9 x $2,600).

* Total estimated value of impact—$93,900
* Costs for Eva and staff (includes travel, lodging, salary, pro-rata
  meeting time and materials costs, etc.)—$11,200
* Return on training—$82,700
* Per person four return—$20,675

What Helped and What Did Not

Contributors

* New computers and access to software provided by county office
* New audit report format instituted by regional director
* Permission for four staff to attend meeting

Barriers

Several planned meetings were rescheduled without notification or
input from professional staff by "emergency" reports required by
county office

Support staff do not receive any incentive or reward for taking on
new responsibilities; local incentives, etc., forbidden by ABC rules.

In this case, dollar values for the impact of the innovation were relatively easy to calculate using figures and data that were available from
the agency. Notice that we took pains to use estimates and calculations
that were in common use within the agency. In this particular agency,
adoption rates (the contribution of money by sponsors to support a
needy child) were known to be linked to the backlog of outbound communications. That is, when field offices were late or negligent in being

sure that "adopted" children sent letters to their sponsors, the responsorship rate was dramatically and negatively impacted. According to our information collection during the Impact Model phase of this SC study, we learned that "backlog reduction" was the bane of field office existence and the mantra sung by the senior leadership. Armed with this knowledge, we scoured our survey results to find cases where backlog reductions had been reported, then made sure that these reductions were real and attributable to the management assistance program during the interview phase.

Figure 6.6 shows a third and final example of an Impact Profile. In this instance, the setting is a large Fortune 100 telecommunications company that had introduced a new program of online tools to help supervisors be more effective. Dramatic growth of the company had spurred a need to promote many new supervisors, many with little experience. At the same time, the demands for effective supervision had escalated dramatically, as production was increasing to meet growing customer orders, and the company was subject to "raiding" by competitors wanting to hire away their technical talent. Recent research in the company showed that retention of staff was directly related to the quality of relationships with supervisors. In this case, we found dozens of positive Success Case stories. Table 6.1 related one of these that was especially poignant, as it showed how "soft skills" were crucial to successful retention and avoidance of costly litigation, and at the same time, could be supported by the resources the company made available to new supervisors.

Figure 6.6 Impact Profile Example for Supervisory Support Tools Program

Impact Example 1—Proactively Resolving a Potential Sexual Harassment Problem

This Impact example describes a success case in which an IT Help Desk manager used the online company policy regarding sexual harassment, the discussion and role plays on this issue from the online *Supervisor Effectiveness (SE)* course, and the "reaching agreement" tools provided to:

Identify and intervene in a potentially negative work place issue

Keep team morale and environment positive and nonthreatening

Impact at a Glance

Immediate Outcomes

- Sexually inappropriate comments not tolerated
- Situation handled in such a way as to prevent any work relationship problems for all parties involved
- All involved employees continue to make very positive contributions to Core, Inc.

Organizational Impact

- Work team productivity kept at very high levels
- Litigation made unnecessary
- Core, Inc., values and culture reinforced

The Impact Story
The supervisor in this situation had thirty-plus direct reports, all who worked in close proximity in an open work environment. Shortly after participating in the SE support program, the manager hired two male, just-out-of -college graduates and, at the same time, a female with experience from another company. About two weeks after their hire, one of the male hires, whose workspace was immediately behind the female hire's space, made a sexually suggestive comment to his female colleague. He proceeded to share this incident with his college buddy who also made an inappropriate comment to this female colleague.

Figure 6.6 Impact Profile Example for
Supervisory Support Tools Program *(continued)*

About a week later, the female hire casually mentioned the incident to the manager. She was quick to point out that she was not mentioning this to get her male colleagues in trouble, only to make the manager aware of the situation. The manager, remembering both Core Inc.'s desire for a sexual harassment-free work environment, decided that he must take action.

He first went to the online supervisory Help section to review Core Inc.'s sexual harassment policy. Next, he downloaded learning materials from the SE course and reviewed the contents regarding sexual harassment. He specifically reviewed a role-play disc and found that useful for planning his next steps.

He then developed a full action plan for resolving this situation. In a full staff meeting, he would review Core Inc.'s sexual harassment policy and describe appropriate and inappropriate actions or comments in this area. Then he planned to meet one-on-one with the two male offenders to set very clear goals about their behaviors related to this issue. He then planned to monitor this situation carefully over time. With his plan in hand, he met with his human resources manager to review his plan and get her feedback. She helped him refine his plan and had him run through exactly what he planned to say in the team and individual meetings. Thus prepared, the manager implemented his plan.

The manager indicated that he is very confident that his message regarding sexual harassment came through loud and clear to all staff members. He said that people are more thoughtful before making comments that others might find offensive. He also said that there were no negative repercussions on the work environment in that the two male colleagues did not feel targeted or embarrassed. The female colleague was not made to feel like a "tattletale" and agreed that the situation, although unfortunate, had been successfully resolved to her satisfaction.

When asked about the potential business impact to Core Inc., of situations like this one, the company attorney noted that "Sexual harassment problems and litigation could cost the company anywhere from thousands to millions of dollars to settle. In addition, no one ever figures the negative publicity costs of such a situation." The supervisor learned that the work environment experiencing sexual harassment charges is extremely toxic. Work teams in such situations suffer from low morale and productivity. "I had a responsibility to not let those things happen at Core Inc. The SE tools helped me navigate my way through this situation confidently."

**Figure 6.6 Impact Profile Example for
Supervisory Support Tools Program** *(continued)*

What Helped. And What Did Not.
Contributors
- Recent training in how to use the Supervisor Effectiveness Toolkit
- Key content from the SE Toolkit
  - Core Inc.'s sexual harassment policy online
  - The sexual harassment role play, skill practice, and feedback in the online module
- A supportive and experienced human resources manager
- A supervisor who understood the potential impact of a harassment event

Barriers
- None identified

Hopefully, these examples of success stories will help readers see the sort of information that must be collected during the interviews. Notice that information presented is factual and dispassionately presented, much as a journalist would report a story. Success stories should "tell it like it is," citing facts and details as necessary to bolster claims of impact and add credibility and interest.

Notice also that no nonsuccess stories are provided as examples. We typically do not write up nonsuccesses as "stories," instead summarizing and explaining (in the final report) the sorts of barriers and issues that nonsuccessful users experienced. In some cases, however, we have found stories of nonsuccess to be so characteristic of critical issues in an organization that we write them as full stories, much like the examples provided in this chapter. Where this reporting will help accomplish the purposes for the evaluation, then by all means nonsuccess stories should be told.

Impact Profiles are typically included in the final SC report and are often the bulk of the report. But, the final report contains other pertinent SC information as well, as we will see in the next chapter.

7.

Communicating Credible and Compelling Results that Tell the Story

Once you have collected your SC information (survey and interview), it is now time to make use of the results. This chapter provides guidance in the creation and communication of Success Case study reports. The aim of the chapter is to help readers create SCM study reports that are compelling and useful—reports that will drive not just understanding of results but help people to take action based on those results. Almost always, a Success Case study discovers information that suggests that changes are needed, such as making revisions to strengthen program process-es, recognizing achievements, extending program services to more people, or perhaps even halting a program that is not accomplishing its intended benefits.

This chapter reviews the major types of purposes and questions an SC study is typically designed to pursue, which were presented in the first chapter of the book, then describes how the reporting step is structured to address each purpose and question. Examples of SC reports are provided to illustrate these where appropriate. Special attention is paid to the sort of analysis of survey findings that will have to be completed and how these survey findings can be combined with Success Case interview information to arrive at final conclusions and recommendations.

Most, but not all, SC studies will culminate in the preparation of a final report that can be distributed to interested audiences, though this is not always the case. In some instances, especially where the SC Method was used as an informal tool to help further develop a program, all that is needed is to capture the essence of the success cases that were discovered. This can be done by writing up each of the Impact Profiles (see Chapter Six for examples), or otherwise preparing them in a communicable format, such as a video, CD, or audiotape.

Very often, however, a final report will be needed to summarize the study and communicate conclusions and recommendations to a broader audience. Thus, most of this chapter is devoted to describing and providing examples of SC analysis and conclusion reports. Although none of these should be treated as "cookbook" prescriptions, readers will find sufficient guidance among them to create their own useful and informative report formats. The final section of the chapter presents and discusses some alternative methods for engaging stakeholders in understanding and applying the results of an SC study. Finally, a mock-up of an SC study report is discussed in the appendix to the book, as well as instructions on where to find the full study report.

The Six Major Success Case Report Conclusions

Although each SC study is unique and has its own particular purposes and constraints, it is useful to consider six major types of conclusions that an SCM study aims to report. Each of these major conclusions entails a different sort of analysis of SCM study data, which is further explained in this chapter. You should also note that these major types of conclusions are not mutually exclusive, as they are usually combined to meet the needs of any particular SC study. These six major types of report conclusions are presented and discussed following, arrayed in order from simple to more complex.

1. *What worthwhile actions and results, if any, is the program helping to produce?* This simplest of SC purposes is to quickly gather evidence about the most poignant and compelling actions and results that a change initiative is producing and provide rich illustrations of these "best case" applications and outcomes.

2. *Are some parts of the program working better than others? Rarely do all parts of a program work equally well.* This sort of analysis and conclusion aims to compare and contrast the several program elements, identifying those that were used especially fruitfully, those that were less used, those used not at all, and so forth. We might conclude, for example, that some program services or tools accounted for almost all of the worthwhile results, while other tools were used only rarely. In the evaluation of an emotional intelligence training program, for example, our analysis showed that one program module (using emotional intelligence skills in conducting client meetings) was used by almost all of the new financial advisors.

3. *What work environment factors are helping support success, and what factors are getting in the way?* This SC analysis identifies and explains those workplace and performance support system factors that are associated with success or nonsuccess. Very often, for example, participants who were especially successful encountered some unusual circumstances or were provided with some unique opportunities or support that other less successful participants did not experience. Similarly, nonsuccessful participants may have encountered certain barriers that differentiated them from more successful participants. In the laptop evaluation, for example, successful users were provided with a level of supervisory support and encouragement that others did not enjoy. In the evaluation of automobile dealerships referred to earlier, we found that dealerships that reaped worthwhile results had provided their salespeople with a compensatory sales commission. That is, salespeople who took time off the sales floor to participate in the televised technical support process were entitled to a share of sales commissions that were earned while they were absent. In dealerships where participation was low, the opposite factor was found; here, salespeople who took time off the floor to engage in the televised program were punished by a reduction in sales commission, thus dramatically suppressing participation.

4. *How widespread is the scope of success?* This sort of SC study provides estimates about what numbers and proportions of program participants are using program services and tools to achieve worthwhile results. For example, we might analyze SC data to conclude that "Sixty percent of the participants used the laptop computers to accomplish worthwhile results that are either helping to drive more new sales, retain customers, or increase

revenues-per-customer. Of these successful participants, one out of five (20%) have achieved profit margins in excess of the company's goal of 15%. On the other hand, 28% of the program's participants have reported no use of the laptops at all and are likewise achieving no impact on sales, retention, or revenue. The remaining 12% have reported some success, but their accomplishments are below profit margin expectations."

5. *What is the ROI (return-on-investment) of the new program?* In many cases, it is possible to use the SC Method to easily and realistically estimate the dollar-value of the successful results being achieved. These can then be compared to the costs of the program, and an ROI estimate can be made.

6. *How much more additional value could be derived from the program?* This SC purpose builds on the ROI calculation to produce an estimate of the "unrealized value" of the program. To pursue this sort of conclusion, the SC study must first document evidence that the program is capable of producing valuable results. We then go further to compare the proportion of people who are using the program to achieve these results to the proportion of people who are not. From this comparison, we are able to estimate how much more value the program could add if more of the nonparticipants were to make use of program services, tools, and so forth. In the evaluation of the emotional intelligence training, for example, we found that some new financial advisors made use of their new skills to their sales appointments. But although the increase in sales appointments was significant (nearly double the rate of appointments), only a small percentage was using the skills in this way. It was quite clear that if more advisors were to apply emotional intelligence skills in appointment-seeking then more

appointments could be made overall. Because prior research in the company showed that a predictable proportion of appointments turned into actual sales, a "business case" could be made for trying to get more new advisors to use emotional intelligence in their quest to make initial client appointments.

As noted, any particular Success Case study will usually combine several of these types of conclusion analyses into its final report. Typically, the more complex the purpose for the study, the more these analyses will be combined. A simple SC study, for instance, might report only on the nature of program usage and results. Beyond this most simple report, we might include an analysis of the scope of the program's impact. In more formal and complex evaluation studies, we often include all of the types of conclusions. In the evaluation of the automobile dealerships, for example, we included an analysis of the factors that impeded usage of the televised technical assistance and reported also on the unrealized value that could accrue if more dealerships made more use of the program services. This information was combined to make recommendations as to how nonparticipating dealerships could be enticed to join in program services and what sorts of proven practices could help dealerships not achieving satisfactory benefit get greater return on their participation investment.

It should be noted that these six types of conclusions are representative and not exhaustive. Further, any particular SC study usually combines two or more of these purposes.

The Conclusion Types Illustrated

This next section of the chapter provides an illustration of each major Success Case study conclusion. Each illustration is briefly described, then examples of pertinent final report elements are presented and discussed.

Conclusion Type 1: The Simple Identification and Description of Program Usage and Results

The final report process for this, the simplest of the SC purposes, is likewise simple. Typically, all that is done at the reporting stage is to produce the Success Case stories (see the examples of Impact Profiles in Chapter Six) and determine an effective way of disseminating them to key audiences. In a written report, the report would consist primarily of the Impact Profiles, along with an explanation of the study's methods.

The table of contents for this simple SC report is shown in Table 7.1.

Table 7.1

Typical Table of Contents for a Simple SC Study

Executive summary	This consists of one to two pages that summarize the purposes and method for the study and includes key excerpts from the Impact Profiles that best illustrate the nature and scope of impact.
Methods	This is a detailed (two to three pages maximum) explanation of the study's methods, highlighting the purpose for the study, timing, when and how a survey was conducted, how many Success Case prospects were interviewed, and so forth. This section should briefly but completely inform a reader as to how the study was organized and conducted, by whom, and under what auspices and authority.
Impact Profiles	This is the bulk of the report—a collection of the most illustrative and dramatic stories of successful applications and results. Each Impact Profile, as seen in Chapter Six, is about one to two pages in length.

Table 7.1 *(continued)*
Typical Table of Contents for a Simple SC Study

Summary and conclusions	It may be that the SC Impact Profiles speak for themselves and require no further discussion. On the other hand, it may be that there are generalizations to be made about similarities and differences among the impact and benefits of the program, characteristics of users who typified success, and so on. If this is the case, a section such as this may be useful.

Conclusion Type 2: Identification of Program Parts that Are Working and Those that Are Not

This sort of analysis and conclusion is important when an SC customer is hoping to improve a program. We especially include this sort of conclusion when we are applying the SCM to a pilot program, as we are always quite sure that some parts of the pilot will have better impact than others.

When the several parts of the program can be clearly identified and differentiated, such as a program that has provided different tools, then the survey itself (as developed from the Impact Model) can ask respondents to report which tools they have used and which they have not. In our evaluation of the supervisory support system at Core Inc., for example, we asked supervisors to indicate which of the several online services they had accessed and which they had not. We were then able to make follow-up interview calls to potential success cases who had reported usage of each of the several tools. In evaluation studies where there is less-clear differentiation among the categories of program services or for other reasons (e.g., to be kept brief) the survey did not assess usage of different services or tools, inquiry into what was used and what was not used takes place in the interviews. That is, we would first identify potential success cases; these are the people who reported achieving valuable results regardless of what particular program element they used. Then, in the interviews, we carefully probe to identify and explain exactly what they used and what they did not.

In the laptop program, for example, the survey data showed high impact for several key outcome categories, such has acquisition of new customers or increased account volume. But it was not until we conducted interviews with these successful people that we found out which laptop applications they actually relied on to help achieve these good results. Because the program initiators really didn't know what might be most useful, they provided quite a few possible application suggestions and supporting software. After they learned from the early users what was working best, later iterations of the laptop program were far more focused, which helped reduce user-frustration, speeded up the training, and got quicker results.

Conclusion Type 3: Identification of Factors that Help or Impede Impact

This type of conclusion grows directly from the previous sort of conclusion that has estimated the scope of impact. Assuming that there is a relatively low positive scope, thus creating room for significantly greater impact, this sort of conclusion may be called for. That is, if a program is achieving significant value for some proportion of trainees but there is a significant proportion of participants who are not achieving results of value, then it may well make sense to try to figure out why it works for some but not for others.

A recent SC evaluation of a technical training program in a large computer company tells this story nicely:

One part of XP Computing (a fictitious name for a large computing services company) sells and services very large and expensive communications servers. Because its server customers—airlines, nationwide stockbrokers, and so forth—have stringent demands for performance and reliability, the company provides a rigorous training program in server installation and initialization for its field service technicians. The training is a two-week "residential" program in which technicians travel to a single West Coast location and stay in a local hotel for the duration of the training. Needless to say, the training is very expensive, consuming a lot of valuable time. Our SC study survey results showed that, of 200 technicians who had attended the training, fully 40%, or eighty people, had not used any of their training— none at all! On the other hand, those who did use the training used it very well. In fact, their usage led to significant business results, such as speedy installation of new servers, prompt repairs of problems that could have rapidly grown to be large problems, and averted delays and outages that would have led to costly repairs, even lawsuits. It was clear that the training, when it was used, helped contribute significantly to critical business goals such as customer satisfaction, retention, and new sales.

In sum, it was amply clear that the training was very effective and led to indispensable business results. But it was equally clear that there was huge waste in the training system, as many of the technicians participated in the training apparently had no use for it. Worse, because the training program relied on large and costly simulators, attendance was limited to small numbers and there were waiting lists of participants. Thus, it was also clear that some technicians who really could have used the training were not able to get it because sessions were full, and this in turn had led to customer complaints due to a lack of proficient service.

Because we had also interviewed a sample of the nonusers, our analysis led us quickly to spot the problem. Service district managers were sending technicians to the training when they seemed to have a lull in business, even

*though their districts had no customers who owned the server whose opera-
tion was the subject of the training! When we followed up to find out why this
practice was happening, we discovered that there was a rational explanation
for this strange behavior. Some of these district mangers sent technicians to
training as a sort of "inoculation" strategy; just in case their district did
acquire a customer with this server, then they would have a trained techni-
cian ready to go. Another reason why managers sent people to the training
was that they did not trust the sales projections that the sales division sent
them. Even though there were no sales of the server projected for customers
in their district, they thought there might possibly acquire a customer with
this particular server, and again, they wanted to be ready with a trained tech-
nician. Unfortunately, their strategy was not working, as the Success Case
study also showed that, unless the technical skills were put to use within a few
weeks after the training, the skills rapidly deteriorated. Worse yet, the strategy of filling training slots with people who did not need it displaced technicians who really did need the training, and the net effect on customer service—the very need for the training in the first place—was negative.*

*It was readily apparent to us that the training itself was just fine and
worked well. All of the problems came from the training selection and fulfill-
ment process. We strongly recommended that the results of the study be
shared with district managers and the sales division. Because cost contain-
ment was such a high priority across this large company in the highly
competitive computer market, our report got acute attention. Steps were
immediately taken to make the selection process more stringent, thus assur-
ing that only those technicians with server customers filled the precious slots
in the training. Steps were also taken to build the credibility of the sales projections, reducing district managers' anxieties about not being able to provide
skilled service when it was needed. Once the right people, and only the right
people, got into the sessions, the impact rate was raised to 100%, and there
was greater customer satisfaction as a result.*

Notice that this sort of conclusion requires inquiry into nonsuccesses as well as successes. Further, this sort of study analysis requires a bit of "detective" work to figure out the reasons for nonsuccess. That is, once we realized from the survey data that there was a large proportion of technicians who reported not to have used their training at all, we immediately focused our follow-up interviews to determine why this was the case. It struck us (and our client) as strange that tightly focused and specialized technical training such as this would have such a high rate of nonusage. But these sorts of conclusions are almost always quite readily available if the SC study director is willing to dig a little, and they often have great value as they can salvage increased value from partially or marginally successful programs.

In another study, for example, we studied the effectiveness of the transition to a team approach to selling, an innovation that was replacing an organization built around single-person sales representatives. Only a few of the teams were successful in achieving higher sales, but most struggled; their costs of sales were higher due to more time spent in the sales process, and their sales performance was not improved. In this study, we were able to identify the key factors that differentiated the successful from the nonsuccessful teams. The organization then took steps to help nonperforming teams learn from and master the techniques and tools that the successful teams were using, and overall performance began to improve.

Conclusion Type 4: Scope of Impact

Fulfilling this conclusion purpose always requires that the SC study has employed a survey, and that either all of the participants, or carefully constructed samples of them, were surveyed. This purpose goes beyond simple illustration of impact to make estimates as to how many or what proportion of participants achieved impact similar in quality and value to the impact that has been illustrated in the Impact Profiles. This report may also characterize the scope of impact for each of several different participant groups, explaining, for example, that the nature and scope of impact was different for different groups of participants.

The basis for this sort of analysis is the survey data. In studies where samples of participants were surveyed, versus all possible participants, then inferential statistics are applied to the survey results to make estimates of impact.

To illustrate this type of conclusion, we will refer again to the example of the program that provided laptop computers to sales representatives. Imagine for purposes of this example that the study was based on and collected the following data:

- A total of 500 representatives were provided laptop computers.
- Our survey was sent to a random sample of 220 of these sales reps, and we had usable survey responses from 200 reps.
- Of these 200 respondents, eighty, or 40%, scored in the highest impact category and were thus identified as possible success cases.
- Fifty respondents, or 25%, reported very little or no usage of their laptops at all and were thus in the lowest category.
- The remaining seventy participants (35%) either reported some minor success or other partial use of their laptops but had not yet used them in the highest-leverage sales applications.

To proceed with our detailed analysis, we drew a random sample of twenty participants from the eighty people comprising the highest scoring category. That is, at random, we chose twenty of the eighty possible success cases for an interview and completed an interview with all of these people. Consider now that, of these twenty people interviewed, eighteen of them (90% of the total of twenty) turned out to be "true positives"; that is, of the twenty, eighteen were actually verified to have achieved results of significant value to the company through use of their laptops. With the remaining two, we were unable to confirm that these people were truly successful and thus could not count them as an actual success cases.

Given this information, we were able to extrapolate estimates of how widespread the success of this program most likely was. Because both the initial survey sample was randomly drawn and the subsequent sample of possible success cases was likewise randomly drawn, the rules of inferential statistics allowed us to make estimates of the impact on the total population of participants within known limits of probable certainty.*

Table 7.2 presents the findings we were able to conclude about the probable scope of impact of this program, and it also includes an explanation of the rationale and basis for the finding.

Table 7.2
Explanation of Example Findings About Scope of Impact

Conclusion	Basis for Conclusion
The laptop program has helped a total of 180 participants to be successful in using their laptops and achieve results of significant value to the business. This represents 36% of the 500 sales reps who were initially provided a laptop.	Why 180 successful participants? Eighty of the 200 sampled participants reported successful results. This was 40% of the sample. A random sample of twenty of these eighty participants were interviewed and, of these, eighteen turned out to be actual successes. Thus, we can conclude that 90% of the participants who reported high success on their survey were true successes. Inferring back to the original population of 500 laptop participants, we can safely estimate that 90% of 40% (or 36%) of the entire population are probably successful users achieving significant results. Thirty-six percent (36%) of 500 = 180.

---

* For readers unfamiliar with the concepts and application of simple inferential research methods and statistics, reference to an expert and/or a standard research test is advised. See the References section at the end of the book for suggestions.

Table 7.2 *(continued)*

Explanation of Example Findings About Scope of Impact

Conclusion	Basis for Conclusion
	How do we know the results were in fact "significant"? First, the survey items were based on the initial Impact Models that our stakeholders had agreed defined success operationally as certain specific achievements. Secondly, we verified the actual business value of these achievements during the interviews.
One hundred twenty-five of the original 500 participants have been unable to use their laptops in any productive applications.	Twenty-five percent of our random sample reported little to no use of the laptops and no significant results. Inferring to the total population, we estimate that 25% of them (25% of 500 = 125) are experiencing no success at all.
The remaining 172 participants were not able to definitively achieve any significant business results from their laptop usage, though they had tried to use them in several different ways. Although some if not many of these participants may eventually use their laptops productively, at this time no significant business value has been realized.	Thirty-five percent of our sample reported only minor usage leading to no significant results (35% of 500 = 172).

As Table 7.2 shows, estimates of scope of impact are relatively easy to extrapolate from survey findings, and these can be further explained and corroborated from the interviews. The credibility and validity of these extrapolations is based on the soundness of the survey itself and the sampling and administration method. That is, if one can attack the survey as an unreliable measure or argue that it is invalid because the items do not represent worthwhile results, then of course the extrapolations themselves come under question. Likewise, if samples were not truly random, or it can be shown that respondents did not answer truthfully or without bias, then the findings are again open to question. But, when the following conditions are met, these sorts of conclusions are logical and defensible:

1. The survey has been clearly and specifically based on an Impact Model that has been agreed upon and verified as faithfully representing the sought for results.
2. The survey instrument itself meets minimum standards for good practice.
3. The sampling and survey methods are technically sound.

Conclusion Type 5: Estimating ROI

Return-on-investment estimates simply take the previous estimates of scope of impact a step further and attach dollar-values to the results reported. For the sake of simplicity and ease on the reader's imagination, the same laptop example described previously will be used. For purposes of this illustration, the ROI claims build on the same data already reported in Table 7.2.

Assume that the survey of laptop usage reported impact claims in each of three impact categories: new sales to new accounts, increased revenues from existing accounts, and increased speed in shipping orders to customers, which is known to be a factor in customer satisfaction that bears on retention of customers. Assume further that the company already had some estimates (which it did) about the business value of these results. That is, an increase in new sales can be shown to be worth $5 in net profit for every $100 of sales revenues. Increased revenues from current customers yields a margin of $10 for every $100, and increased speed in shipping is estimated to account for 20% of customer retention (a value on average of $500 per order, based on estimates of what it costs to acquire a new customer).

Using these figures and the most conservative estimation formulas (verified by the accounting department at the company), we were able to report that, on average, successful usage of laptops led to benefits worth $5,000 per sales representative per quarter, or $20,000 per year. It cost only $6,000 per sales rep to equip and train the reps in the use of a laptop Thus, for those sales reps using their laptops effectively, the program was clearly returning a significant amount of benefit relative to its cost—more than a three-fold increase. Recall, however, that not all sales reps were using their laptops this successfully. In fact, only 36% of the reps—180 in all—were estimated to be this successful.

Because the remaining 64% were not apparently achieving any worthwhile benefits at all, the overall ROI of the program is estimated to be far less. It cost the company $300,000 to equip and train all 500 sales reps with the laptops. Of these 500, 180 appeared to be achieving value worth about $360,000 per year ($20,000 times eighty sales reps using the laptops successfully). Thus, overall and to date, the laptop program was little more than paying for itself. Importantly, however, there appeared to be a lot more benefit that the program could achieve if only more sales reps could be helped to use their laptops! This fact takes us neatly to the sixth general SC conclusion category: estimating the unrealized value in an initiative that could, if leveraged, increase the scope and depth of impact.

Conclusion Type 6: Estimating Unrealized Value

This conclusion purpose involves making estimates of how much more value a program could be achieving, based on the value it is currently achieving. This purpose comes especially into play when the following four conditions are met:

1. Only a very few—a small proportion—of the participants are making successful use of a change initiative.
2. Those few who are using the innovation are doing so with great success worth significantly more than the individual cost of engaging each one in the innovation.
3. The SC study has identified some of the key factors that differentiate a successful from a nonsuccessful performer.
4. At least some of these factors could be relatively easily managed to overcome their negative effect.

We refer jokingly to this scenario as the "consultant's dream," because the conditions so readily justify a proposal for a further intervention to help more participants use the innovation successfully! It is already known that the innovation, when used, leads to significant results. But only a few are using it in this way, thus there is a seemingly great upside potential for greater overall value if only more participants could use the innovation. Finally, because we know which factors (if manipulated differently) could increase success and we have some suggestions for helping manipulate them effectively, we have the makings for an easy business-case to justify a recommendation for further intervention. In this scenario, it is a relatively simple matter to estimate how many more participants we would have to help use the innovation successfully to justify the costs of our proposed intervention.

Again, it will be useful to return to the laptop example, as most of the information we need to understand this example has already been provided. Assume that we have identified three key factors that differentiated a successful from a nonsuccessful laptop owner. These are: (1) a certain version of software that is easier to use, (2) a manager who is computer-savvy and is willing to provide coaching, and (3) a certain fundamental ability in mathematical operations or access to a resource that can help with these calculations.

Assume further that we have proposed to do three things: get everyone the better software, provide computer training to managers who need it, and install an easy-to-use mathematical calculator program on each sales rep's laptop who feels he or she needs it. As a part of this proposed action, we will also make all managers and sales reps aware of the nature and significance of our SC study results, so they know how to leverage these new resources for maximum benefit.

Table 7.3 provides an overview of the final report conclusions and their rationales for this laptop usage scenario.

Table 7.3
Example Conclusions that Estimate Unrealized Value from a Laptop Computer Initiative

Conclusion	Explanation
At a maximum, this program could lead to $640,000 in additional bottom-line value.	Of the total 500 participants, 320 (500 minus 180) are not using their laptops for business value. If these 320 sales reps could use their laptops as well as the 180 best users, the return benefit would be $640,000 ($20,000 per sales rep).[1]
A more reasonable goal for increased value might be $160,000.	If we could get just half the nonuser sales reps to use the laptops half as well as the 180 best, this would lead to $160,000 in bottom-line impact (one-half of 320 = 160 sales reps). One hundred and sixty sales reps achieving increased value of $10,000 (one-half of $20,000, the value achieved by the best users) equals $160,000.

[1] This estimate assumes that there is a market potential for an increase of sales to the level required to produce these net results. In this case, the director of sales confirmed that the market indeed provided this much room, and more, for increasing sales by taking market share away from competitors.

Table 7.3 (*continued*)
**Example Conclusions that Estimate Unrealized Value
from a Laptop Computer Initiative**

Conclusion	Explanation
A proposal to achieve the $160,000 noted increase in usage could achieve an ROI of 500%.	To train the managers and install the two necessary software upgrades would cost $32,000. By the estimates above, a modest goal, this should lead to $160,000 in bottom-line benefits. Even if this proposal is only half as effective as we think it will be, it will still achieve an ROI of 250%.

Building Interest in SC Study Findings

One major and enduring challenge for any sort of organizational analysis and inquiry is trying to get key people and groups to pay attention to findings. This is likewise true of an SC study. Of course, when the study is small and informal, perhaps being done only to satisfy the curiosity of the few people leading the study, this should not be a daunting challenge, because the study audience and the study leaders are one and the same people. In a larger SC study, however, we always have to look ahead and strategize early on the best means to employ to get our key audiences to pay attention to and consider our SC findings.

The SC Method has some major natural advantages in meeting the "attention" challenge. First, the output of an SC study consists primarily of stories, and these are often naturally interesting and compelling. Thus, one strategy for getting attention is to highlight and otherwise put the stories at the forefront of reporting methods. We often select one of the most intriguing stories and put it at the very front of the report, perhaps as a preface. Or, if the report is using an oral presentation format, we start the presentation with the most interesting story.

The SC Method is also relatively quick, because it is not overly complex or broad in scope. SC study leaders can begin providing their results in a matter of weeks after starting a study, thus "striking while the iron is hot," presenting results before the attention of stakeholders has migrated to a new concern. To take advantage of this, we always do our best to achieve the shortest possible turnaround time in an SC study, unless there is some other advantage to be gained by delaying a final report, such as waiting for an already-scheduled meeting that offers an advantageous forum.

Even with these natural advantages, though, an SC study can fall prey to a lukewarm or uninterested reception. Sometimes this lack of attention is neutral and passive, due to nothing more than people's busy-ness and being overwhelmed with additional concerns. In other instances an unwillingness to embrace study findings is due to a disposition to disagree with findings that do not align with already-formed opinions and biases. Or, lack of attention to study findings may be more sinister, where those who reject or resist conclusions and recommendations are doing so out of political interests, "turf protection," or other self-serving agendas.

It is never possible to assure that all stakeholders will warmly and enthusiastically embrace evaluation findings. In fact, when the importance of a program is quite high, and the evaluation findings are quite strong (either positive or negative), you can be quite sure there will be some degree of strife. Those who have political stock in the success of the program venture will warmly greet positive findings and will be very skeptical of negative findings. Those who are enemies of the new program will behave in a similar manner, though in the opposite direction. The best that an evaluation team can do is, before the evaluation, try to surface and understand all political stakes (pro and con), design instruments and measurement procedures with care, and most importantly, involve key stakeholders in every step of the design process. After the evaluation has concluded, it is good practice to give advance warning to stakeholders of especially strong positive or negative findings and help them understand these findings and begin to think about how they can positively apply them.

Whatever the circumstances of the evaluation, it is always good practice to do your best to get the highest degree of involvement in understanding and applying the findings of the evaluation that you possibly can.

Table 7.4 provides a listing of the key tactics we employ to get the greatest attention to SC study findings.

Table 7.4
Tactics for Getting Attention to SC Study Findings

Tactic	Explanation
Use a variety of report formats keyed to audience interests	We may include the following types of report formats in a single evaluation:
	Executive summary (one to two pages maximum) for senior level audiences
	Detailed report for stakeholders with management responsibility for the program being studied
	Brief article for newsletters or other internal and external public relations vehicles
Consider alternative media articles, dramatic skits, for the report	Use meetings, workshops, "magazine" video and audiotapes, and other creative media formats and outlets for your findings. Videotape or live presentations by success cases are especially powerful.

Table 7.4 *(continued)*

Tactics for Getting Attention to SC Study Findings

Tactic	Explanation
Conduct a workshop for key stakeholders to discuss and apply findings	We always include a workshop in a proposal to conduct an SC evaluation. We provide every attendee with a preliminary summary report (brief), then conduct a workshop wherein we present findings, I head discussions about the findings, and if agreed to, have small groups of participants work to apply findings and make recommendations for action.
Involve stakeholders in SC study steps	Always allow your stakeholders to review and critique evaluation instruments. Provide them with preliminary "draft" reports to get their suggestions for correction of errors, oversights, and so forth.

Invite some stakeholders to participate in data collection and analysis activities. We sometimes have client representatives help conduct interviews and/or sit in on analysis meetings when we are discussing Success Case cut-off scores, interview protocol drafts, and so forth.

For a complete example of an SC study final report, readers are referred to the appendix. This provides information to find a complete report for an actual SC study conducted by the author and his colleagues. The report has been sanitized only to the extent that the name of the real client organization has been changed; otherwise, it is complete as it was originally written and provided to the client.

8.

Putting the Success Case Method to Work: Strategic Applications

Evaluation in general has a range of purposes, such as to justify program expenditures, promote accountability, help make decisions about whether to extend, curtail, or revise a program, and so forth. The SCM is a useful approach whenever there is an interest in assessing and learning about how well a program is working or whether it is achieving the goals and benefits that were intended. So, whenever there is an evaluative interest in impact or questions about how well some innovation is working, the SCM is a possible choice.

We can use the SCM, for example, with the "at risk" program that is undergoing unusual scrutiny. Sometimes, a program is in the "hot seat," drawing critical attention from a number of audiences, some of whom may be especially skeptical. The SCM works especially well here, because it can produce data relatively quickly and because it can yield clear and specific examples of results and benefits. Demands for accountability are also a common driver of evaluation applications. These demands can spring from any number of political, market, or organizational forces. That is, a program might be called on to demonstrate accountability in times of decreasing resources and greater budget pressures. Or, a reorganization (such as during a merger) may require that some programs that are possibly duplicate in nature be investigated to assess how well they work and what value they really add. Whenever forces conspire to require a review of how well a program is working, whether it is working, what sort of value it is contributing, and so forth, then the SCM is a logical choice.

But the SCM is probably most valuable as part of a larger organizational change and improvement strategy. As organizational change leaders, we are all stuck in the same boat of having insufficient and incomplete knowledge as to what exactly needs to be done to improve organizational effectiveness. Although a client, for example, may be 100% right knowing they need to do something to improve sales performance, they will rarely be anywhere 100% correct as to exactly what needs to be done to achieve that goal. Rapid change, incomplete knowledge of cause–effect relationships, insufficient information about what is really happening, misleading data, and the pressure for a quick response all conspire to make our solutions less than perfect. And, of course, even if our solution were perfect, when it was designed (which it is not), by the time it got delivered into the field of the organization, things would have changed to make it less than right at the moment. The reality of organizational change leadership is that we, the leaders and helpers, are always playing with less than a full deck of knowledge. The very best we can do is be partially right. Given that reality, we have to learn quickly what works and what does not, so that we can continuously revise our solutions and build better (though not perfect) solutions for the future based on our learning from the present.

This chapter outlines a number of especially useful and strategic applications of the SCM that aim at improving the effectiveness of organizational change. Although these strategic applications of the SCM are named and described separately in the following sections of this chapter, they are all aimed at the overall goal of accelerating change and organizational learning.

Mining "Gems" from a Large and Mature Program

As noted in the beginning of the book, organizational change initiatives are almost always only partially successful—some parts of them work and some parts of them do not. The Success Case Method can be very useful in sorting the wheat from the chaff in programs, identifying and describing the best that a program is producing. When these few most-productive applications of an initiative are identified, they can be nurtured or otherwise supported so that proportionately more success can be derived from the investment in the program. This strategy is especially useful when applied to large and disparate programs that have been in place a long time and/or have a number of program elements and potential applications. Inevitably, as time goes by, there will be some parts of the program that will become irrelevant, be used incorrectly, or otherwise lose their effectiveness. But, because the larger program is viewed favorably, these less-effective elements survive despite their relative lack of value. American Express Financial Advisors, for example, had provided its well-known program in emotional intelligence for many years, and many employees from a wide range of job roles had participated. Although most people in the company believed in the program and its value, it had been in place long enough to develop a considerable number of skeptics and detractors. There were instances where it had not proved very useful or had not been seen to achieve positive outcomes. The evaluation of this program showed that the detractors were to some extent right; indeed, there were a number of instances in which the emotional intelligence program was not very useful or productive. But the program supporters were also proven correct; there were many cases as well where the program was being very productively used and was leading to quite valuable outcomes. The evaluation was helpful in sorting out and describing those most useful and productive applications of emotional intelligence training and helped American Express identify as well the elements of the program that were not working as planned. As a result, program leaders were able to make revisions to the program to target it on the most productive outcomes and remove or revise those parts that were not working. Further, by identifying the more specific valuable applications of the program, the leaders were able to create more efficient interventions with a tighter and more specific focus. This enabled participants to choose elements that were most relevant to their needs and reduced overall costs while improving impact.

Salvaging Valuable Parts from a Doomed Program

This is a similar scenario where there may be gems to be mined from a program. In this case, however, the larger program has been mostly unsuccessful and is slated to be terminated. Almost always, even though the majority of opinion may rightfully believe that a program is a failure, there will often be some small minority that believes in its value. In these cases, the SCM can be quickly and efficiently deployed to see if the few program supporters have a valid case. It is simply a matter of finding these few supporters and asking them to identify the outcomes that the program is achieving for them. If successes can indeed be identified, they can be described, documented, and analyzed to see if there is anything worth keeping from, or learning about, the program despite its larger and more general failure. In the best-case scenario, there will be a few program applications that are found to be worthwhile, and these can be salvaged and built on.

In one study, for example, we evaluated how well an individual development planning system and tool was working in a large oil company. The development planning process was supposed to be used to create an individual development plan for each employee in the company. All managers at all levels had been provided with the system tools and had received training in their use, but the evaluation showed almost no success at all. Only a very small percentage (less than 8%) of employees had completed the process with their managers and actually completed a development plan. One step in the system process, a meeting to discuss the employees' growth goals, however, had been more broadly applied, though that too was at levels far lower than program leaders had hoped for. Forty percent of employees reported they had initiated a discussion with their manager about their future growth, and they further reported they found this of some value. In interviews we were able to document that these meetings had indeed taken place with some managers and employees, and we were further able to document some valuable outcomes. In some cases, for instance, the meetings resulted in greater understanding of and commitment to unit production goals. In other cases, the manager and the employee identified and resolved misunderstandings that were depressing performance. In yet other cases, the meeting led to mutual decisions about a job reassignment that, if not addressed, would have led to the loss of an employee. In short, the overall program was a failure, but it did provide a tool and method for encouraging and increasing dialogue between managers and their employees, something that was clearly a vital need in this organization. The program leaders gave up on their mission to install a full-blown development planning system but were able (based on the data from the evaluation) to win support for a manager/employee communication initiative. A follow-up evaluation of this program showed a considerable increase in positive communications that were leading to several important outcomes in employee morale, retention, and productivity.

This evaluation had a yet another positive outcome. Though the development planning system was clearly not working, our study of the reasons why it was not working revealed some important information about the general miserable state of manager/employee relations in the company. This led to a better understanding on senior management's part of why the company was facing a loss of personnel and the general lack of trust in management decisions. Although the program was a failure, the attention it focused on poor communications helped the program leaders make a case for more resources to work on this growing problem. This experience helped us confirm our belief that even in the worst-case scenario where the supporters are proven wrong, there may still be valuable learning to be gleaned in discovering why the program did not work at all, even when it had a handful of enthusiastic supporters. Finding out why a program did not work can be just as valuable as finding out why a program worked.

Employing a "Rapid Prototyping" Approach

Rapid prototyping is an approach to marketing that was developed by leaders in the high-technology industry. In the highly competitive personal computer business, for instance, it was clear that the manufacturer who waited to develop a product with all of the features and functionality that customers wanted could lose the market to a competitor who got a similar product to market faster, even though that product might not be exactly complete or perfect. The "rapid prototyping" approach dictates that a new product should be provided as fast as possible even though it may not yet be as complete as what designers know the market wants. The early versions of the product help win buyers, who in turn provide valuable market research to designers who can make iterative improvements based on the user experience of the early purchasers. In this way, the need that consumers have is met right away, though not perfectly. At the same time, developers get to make improvements based on the experience of these first customers

Organizational change leaders can valuably adopt this same approach. Internal performance improvement consultants, for example, have learned that if they do not react immediately to a need to improve performance several bad things can happen. One, their clients will look for someone else who can provide faster service. Two, the performance need goes unmet, which impacts the business negatively. Three, the internal consultant function is viewed (rightfully) as nonresponsive and loses credibility and the right to do future business. On the other hand, if these same consultants adopted a rapid prototyping approach, providing a more immediate service or tool that addresses at least a part of the need, even though it is not a perfect tool, they can reverse these negative outcomes.

The SCM works especially well at promoting a rapid prototyping approach, which we also sometimes call an "emergent design" approach. Accordingly, we encourage our clients to act as fast as they can to provide a service or tool to their customers when a need arises. They should provide this "first generation" service version to that relatively small group of people whose need is most poignant and who are most likely to put it to use right away. Then, a small and rapid SCM study is done with these early adopters of the service to learn what about it works best and what works least. This information can then be used to improve the service or tool for the second wave of users, which is in turn studied with a quick SCM study.

This iterative approach assures both rapid service and a continuously improved effectiveness. In today's environment of increasingly rapid change, the emergent design, rapid prototyping approach makes increasing sense. It acknowledges as well the reality that the complexity of the organizational environment and the rapid changes that it undergoes constantly mean that the cause-effect knowledge base of the service provider will never be sufficient to make a complete or even near-perfect solution. The best that can be done is to incorporate learning (needs analysis) into the solution provision phase, simultaneously helping our clients while learning from them how to better serve them.

Improving a Vital Support Program

Many organizations undertake a dramatically new strategic direction (a new product line, a massive technological innovation, a new market) that, because of their significance and scope, have a number of supporting programs that are necessary to accomplish the strategic shift. Some old-line insurance companies, for example, that had created a strong reputation for their line of insurance products, are now (with banking deregulation) moving into new product lines such as financial planning and mutual funds. This sort of change requires some major redirection and new support, such as training or access to new information systems and market channels. Any of these key support programs are natural targets for evaluation scrutiny, simply because if they are not working well, the success of the entire strategic shift is threatened. Again, the SCM can be very useful in helping to make these vital support programs accomplish what they need to.

It is especially useful to identify those supporting programs that are most needed in the early phases of the implementation of a new change or innovation. A large retail store chain company, for example, was introducing a major change to sell credit products (e.g., credit cards) and other financial services to its customers. The company had a huge and extremely loyal base of customers who, it was thought, could be sold financial services under the company's well-known and deeply respected brand. A part of this larger plan was a relatively simple first step, which was to install an electronic kiosk in each retail store where customers could apply, online, for a company store credit card (seen as the first step in wooing them as financial services customers). Yet to accomplish this first step, the company had to get retail storeowners, almost all of whom were independent owners, to provide the space to install the kiosk. Early results of this effort were disappointing, as many retailers reneged on their promise to install the kiosk or had located it in a less than accessible spot in the store. This small failure threatened to undermine and seriously delay the financial services strategy, which was already being exploited by competitors. This was an especially good opportunity for an SCM study, which could quickly find out, from the early and successful adopters of the kiosk, how they had made it work and overcome what appeared to them to be a loss of otherwise productive retail square footage.

Providing Exemplary Role Models to Teach and Motivate Others

It is a virtual certainty that in any new program some people will do a better job than others of making use of program tolls and resources. A parallel issue is that those who have less success are likely to become discouraged and quit their efforts. Worse yet, they may influence others to give up their attempts or not even try in the first place. A critical mass of unhappy or unsuccessful users can quickly undermine a program. On the other hand, a critical mass of successful users can help a program succeed.

The SCM has been used to quickly root out those most successful users of an innovation before others who are less successful have a chance to do much damage. The experience of the successful adopters can be documented and provided to others to serve as a guide and "role model" that both encourages participation and provides specific guidance as to how to make it work best. Note that these people do not have to be completely successful. They can be only partially successful or have used only some small part of the program's resources to achieve success. The important thing is to find success no matter how small or partial and tell the story of how the innovation can be used and has been used by real people to get worthwhile results.

In a study of pharmaceutical sales representatives, for example, we were investigating how well some new training in interpersonal skills had been used. As it turned out, only one sales rep had used the training successfully. But the application of the training (to influence and gain access to a steering committee at a large health maintenance organization or HMO) turned out to be extremely valuable. This focused and relatively narrow application represented a strategic opportunity for the company, however, because HMO committees could influence dramatic amounts of sales. The SCM study carefully documented this single application and provided detailed information as to exactly what the successful sales rep had done. This information was then provided to other sales reps with similar challenges, leading to a number of large sales.

Marketing an Initiative

A number of our clients have used their SCM to in marketing efforts. That is, they use the SCM to discover and document successful use of a program or innovation, then use these stories of success to influence others to try the program. In fact, over the past few years, a growing number of SCM customers are companies that provide organization improvement and development services, as they find that SCM studies are compelling evidence of the results their interventions can achieve. They provide a further benefit of helping clarify and establish the expectations that the potential "buyer" of the service must commit to provide as well, because a success story also includes a report on the factors that help, or impede, results.

A large telecommunications company, for example, had tried out the services of an online coaching provider in one of its functional units. A number of people were skeptical, however, and doubted that coaching could be provided at a distance, relying only on telephone and email for interaction between the coach and manager. Early in the program, we conducted an SCM study of the coaching intervention and identified several dramatic successes that had led to significant business results. These stories were documented and told in considerable detail, showing first exactly how the manager had used the coaching service, then providing specific evidence of the valuable results that the coaching had led to. Special attention was paid to success in helping achieve business objectives, which pleased senior management, and also in achieving the manager's personal goals (such as reducing anxiety in performance appraisals), which appealed to the prospective coaching customers themselves.

These stories were made available to anyone who was thinking about using the service and were presented in unit work meetings to recruit new customers. Because the success stories were more than mere testimonials and reported substantial evidence of results, they were persuasive in getting new people to try this controversial service. They were also helpful in clarifying and establishing what commitments the user of the service had to make in order to derive benefit from the program. It was clear from the success stories, for instance, that a successful user of coaching was always honest and forthright in reporting actions taken, kept their coaching appointments religiously, and was open to and used feedback from others. Potential users who were not willing to make these commitments were able to opt out of participating. This self-selection and user-awareness and understanding helped to make the program even more successful.

Pinpointing the Specific Value of "Soft" Interventions

Many organizational development leaders are familiar with the objections raised by and the difficulty in selling so called "soft skill" programs and initiatives. Soft skills are those interpersonal and otherwise hard-to-define sorts of capabilities, as opposed to "hard skills" such as computer programming, mechanical abilities, and other technical skills and procedures. When I was an officer in the U.S. Navy, for example, it was quite easy to get approval to train my division personnel on a new piece of sonar equipment. It was easy for anyone to understand why the training was needed, and it was likewise easy to tell if it worked or not (the crew could operate the sonar to detect and classify a target). But, when I tried to make a case that the crew in my division needed communications training, it was difficult to get approval to take them off duty and teach them how to listen, ask questions, and so forth. I could try, as I did, to make the case that things didn't go well during watches and that arguments and misunderstandings interfered with our effectiveness, but I was rarely successful in getting approval.

The common wisdom is that these sorts of soft skill enhancement interventions are hard to measure and rarely get good results. The reason they are both hard to measure and often do not show positive results go hand in hand, of course. First, a soft skill such as communicating lies at the heart of many interactions. To communicate with good results, a person has to deploy different sorts of skills strategically, depending on the circumstance that presents itself. Rarely do training programs and other support tools provide enough specific and personalized practice and feedback to help people improve. Secondly, much of the immediate impact of improved core skills is a subtle reaction on the part of the person being interacted with. Only after these more positive reactions are formed are we likely to see some tangible impact such as an increase in sales, a resolution of a dispute, or so forth. As a result, outcomes of soft skill interventions are likewise seen as soft and not worthwhile.

The SCM has been effectively applied in a number of soft skill interventions and has the advantage of providing specific evidence of the application of a soft skill leading inexorably to a significant outcome. We were able to show in the emotional intelligence training program, for example, that a reported decrease in feelings of rejection led to more persistence in making cold sales calls, which in turn led to more appointments, which in turn led to more sales and revenues. An additional advantage of the SCM is that it shows in detail exactly how and when people have used their soft skill. These specific exemplary applications of the soft skill can be used to help others focus their applications of soft skills in similar, more strategic ways. These specific behavioral examples can be used by trainers and others to demystify soft skills and provide behavioral models to guide further adoption.

Supporting and Leveraging "Pioneer" Experiences

This last strategic application of the SCM to a great extent combines some of the applications already presented. But because it has proven quite successful in the special instance of management and leadership development, I include it here as a separate application. The premise of this application is to accelerate organizational change by launching and nurturing a cadre of "pioneers" who agree to try some new tool, method, or training, despite a lack of proof that it will work or even specific guidance in how to use it.

Consider, for example, our evaluation of a new management development initiative for a national agency that provides services to war veterans. This particular agency program grew from frustration with typical training approaches that provided learning as an "event," wherein service office leaders would attend a two- or three-day training seminar.

Time after time, follow-up studies had shown little impact from such programs. Despite genuine enthusiasm for the tools and methods learned, these one-shot initiatives didn't provide enough sustained inter-action and support to really make a significant difference. These tradi-tional development programs are usually loaded with lots of content and a range of general application examples. Because the designers do not know the specific details of the participants' workplace needs and cir-cumstances, they often compensate with providing many different examples and generic practice exercises, hoping participants will find one or two relevant ideas in the morass of content they provide.

This new program took a starkly different approach. They mini-mized the content and provided only a sketchy orientation to a few key management methods and tools. The assumption was that the partici-pants would generate their own content by trying the new ideas and methods. The process began with a brief meeting at which the new tools (e.g., a problem-solving template) were distributed and briefly explained. Then, participants were asked to return to their offices and, in the next few weeks, try at least one of the tools in some application of their own devising.

At subsequent meetings (which were scheduled for one day each month), a facilitator convened the group and led discussions to explore the experience of each participant, asking specifically what was tried and how well it worked. As time went by, the participants discovered and shared increasingly specific and detailed methods for using the tools to manage important office performance. Parallel with this process, we conducted Success Case simple and fast evaluations. The purpose of the SCM studies was to identify those few and most suc-cessful users of the tools, then help them document and prepare their story for telling at the next meeting of the group.

When we started the process, we knew only that (1) the seminar had provided a handful of specific tools and methods to enhance communications and supervisory effectiveness and (2) that it was purportedly "working," at least for some people. Neither we nor anyone else was able to prescribe or predict how the tools would be used. The program was intentionally vague and indeterminate about how participants might use what the program provided, because this alternative approach was specifically intended to allow the participants to develop their own "content," discovering and refining the particular applications that seemed to work for them.

The study began as a relatively blank slate, and our goal was to find out, through carefully structured inquiry, what were the most productive managerial applications of the tools provided and how (if at all) they were helping to achieve the agency's goals. By the end of the study, we had identified and documented, in considerable detail, a number of successful practices that had been demonstrated to help achieve office goals. These successful practices were detailed in written guides that were then made available to other offices.

In some respects the laptop program described earlier in the book was likewise an example of the pioneer approach. At the beginning of the program, no one knew exactly how the laptops could be used. The few early adopters tried them and discovered some powerful ways in which to use them. These stories of use were then captured in an SCM study and provided to more users. These users formed a second wave of pioneers who in turn discovered new applications at the same time that they refined earlier applications. As time went by, the laptop program became increasingly prescriptive as a database of more certain knowledge developed.

Your Turn

At this point—the end of the book—my wish is that you, the reader, will soon have a success story of your own: How you used the Success Case Method to help accomplish some worthwhile goal.

But where to start? Above all, note that trying out the SCM need not be a massive effort or even a formal evaluation. Of course, if there is a large initiative or a pressing evaluation demand for which the SCM would be helpful, then by all means do not shy away from it. But a small and informal effort is also fine and perhaps advisable. Above all, your first experience with the SCM should be a success, thus it makes sense to keep the project small, focused, and manageable.

A friend, for example, tried out the Success Case approach in a very small but meaningful way with his teenage daughters. I probably appreciate this example to an exceptional degree because I likewise am a father of four, two of whom are still teenagers who would rather do almost anything other than talk with a parent. Having been frustrated by a lack of communication with his daughters, my friend tried a new approach and, at a moment that seemed to lend itself to the likelihood of a conversation, asked one of the girls what she had done that week that was especially rewarding and successful. "Tell me," he asked, "as you look back over your week at school, what of all the things you did, seemed to go the best or make you the happiest?"

Suspicious, the daughter asked, "Is this some kind of trick question, like where you analyze my answer and tell me what's wrong with me? What if what I liked was something just sort of stupid?"

He assured her that any answer was fine with him and that he just wanted to know what she did, no matter how "stupid," that she found especially enjoyable. She told him briefly about a volleyball practice where she was praised by the coach for making a difficult shot. From here, they launched into a conversation that, although it was admittedly brief, at least involved the exchange of a bit of information and allowed him a rare chance to just talk and show an interest in her life.

Now clearly, this was not a Success Case study as it has been presented in this book, but the application of the fundamental principles of the SCM still applied: We can learn something of value by looking at a few, even one, of our most successful endeavors.

In closing, I encourage each reader to find some sort of opportunity in the near future to try out some, if not all, of the SCM process. If you are in the sort of role where evaluation or assessment of organizational initiatives is a part of your normal work, then there should be plenty of such opportunities. For you, an evaluation need that is characterized by a demand to act quickly or a demand to assess simply how well some new initiative is working would be an ideal time to try out a Success Case approach.

For you readers not in the routine business of evaluation, you are seeking a scenario in which you need to learn something, for yourself or others, about what is really happening in a new initiative or how well it is working. Here is a brief example: In my university teaching role, I had introduced a new Web-based coursework process wherein students were to individually complete case study assignments accessed on the Internet, then use email to engage in critical discussion with other classmates. I fully expected that this new endeavor would be variably successful, working fairly well for some but probably not for others. Additionally, I knew that some students might not perform well without the structure and social pressure that a classroom session provided, and others might even shirk the requirement all together.

Soon after we had started the new process, I had each student respond to a brief email message asking them to rate their success in using Web-based assignments. I then contacted a couple of students who reported the greatest success and asked them to prepare a brief presentation for our next class meeting on what they had done and how they had made the Web process work. For those few who had the least success, I asked them to report privately to me what had gone wrong (I did not want to embarrass them with a class presentation demand). I took their comments and made a presentation myself on the barriers and issues confronted by some students. We then spent our next classroom meeting talking about the Web-based assignment process and how it was working. The dialogue that followed these presentations was helpful in two important ways. First, it helped me to restructure the Web process, changing some requirements to make it more simple and attractive. Second, the students learned from both the successes and nonsuccesses some techniques and approaches they could try to increase their success and make the Web-based learning assignments less burdensome and more productive. And last, I learned yet again how usefully and richly we can all learn from our successes and failures.

A Success Case Study Final Report

The appendix presents an actual Success Case study final report and is available as a PDF file from Triad's Web site at www.triadperform.com. To access the report, click "Resources," then "White Papers and Articles." You can also obtain the final report from www.bkconnection.com. The report is provided exactly as it was completed and presented to a client, except that the report has been "sanitized" to remove the actual name of·the company for which the study was conducted.

This report presents the results of an evaluation study that was conducted by Triad Performance Technologies, Inc., a performance improvement and training effectiveness consulting firm in Farmington Hills, Michigan. The study assessed the business impact of training and performance support services that an automobile manufacturer made available to its many dealerships nationwide in the United States. These training programs and support tools were provided to the dealerships over the company's proprietary satellite television network (called here "MortonStar"). The company telecast the courses and performance support tools (e.g., filmed behavioral examples) from its central headquarters in Detroit, Michigan. Dealerships anywhere in the country could tune in to the program from a room in the dealership that was specially equipped to receive and participate in the broadcast using two-way full interactive (voice, visual, and handheld touch-pad response units) capability.

The evaluation reported in this appendix related to two MortonStar courses that were each aimed at increasing the effectiveness of interactions with dealership customers. These two courses were often taken as a combined pair, thus the evaluation sampled from among those participants who had enrolled in both courses.

The overall issue that the automobile company wished to explore was whether participation in the programs contributed to any positive results for dealerships and also what factors and conditions in the dealerships enhanced or suppressed those results. The MortonStar leaders already knew that there was variable participation in the programs, with some dealerships being regular users and others barely ever participating. They knew as well that some dealerships were quite disciplined in their participation, while others took part more casually and sporadically.

The issue of participation and benefits was somewhat complicated by the fact that the company had recently implemented a dealer certification program as part of a global quality assurance and marketing strategy. Accordingly, a dealership could become a "Gold Star" dealership if it met certain company-mandated requirements for procedures and systems, one of which included participation in training by dealership staff. This training certification required various dealership staff (e.g., service writers, salespeople) to complete a certain required set of courses and programs. Most dealerships were anxious to achieve Gold Star status, as this carried with it certain preferential priorities such as reduced loan rates and higher-priority allotments for popular vehicles from the factory. As a result, it was possible that participation in some of the courses could be driven more by a desire to complete certification rather than a need to improve performance of dealership employees.

Part of the motivation for the evaluation was to determine how more dealerships might be enticed to participate in the televised programs. The system that provided these programs (MortonStar) was very expensive and prominent; those who led the MortonStar function were under some pressure to demonstrate its value, and this of course would be helped by more widespread participation among the dealerships. Part of the evaluation was to focus on factors that were related to whether and how much value was gained by a dealership through its participation. If, for example, the evaluation showed that MortonStar participation contributed to valuable dealer business results, then the MortonStar leaders could use this information to market their services. Further, they could use the data from our assessment of enhancing and inhibiting factors to provide suggestions to dealerships as to what actions they could take to use the MortonStar network for the greatest impact.

This evaluation did indeed discover that MortonStar participation, when it was carried out in a disciplined manner, could contribute to particular positive business outcomes related to sales and customer satisfaction. These of course are primary business goals of dealerships, so though impacts were modest (as would be expected from brief and simple training), they were significant. Readers will also note that we were able to pinpoint a few specific dealership actions that promoted impact.

There are two ways to get a copy of the appendix:

- Visit Triad's Web site at www.triadperform.com, then click "Resources" and "White Papers and Articles."
- Or you can obtain the report from www.bkconnection.com.

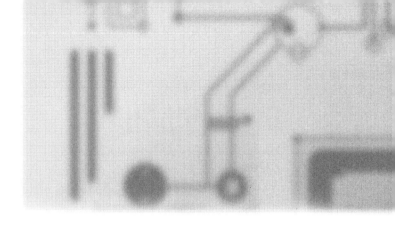

References

Guba, E., and Lincoln, Y. *Naturalistic Inquiry*. Thousand Oaks, CA: Sage. 1985.

Kibel, B. M. *Success Stories as Hard Data: An Introduction to Results Mapping*. New York: Kluwer/Plenum. 1999.

Simmons, A. *The Story Factor*, page 27. Cambridge, MA: Perseus. 2001.

Stake, R. E. *The Art of Case Study Research*. Thousand Oaks, CA: Sage. 1995.

Additional Resources

Inferential Statistics

Levy, S. G. *Inferential statistics in the social sciences*. New York: Holt, Rinehart & Winston. 1968.

Lomax, R.G. *An introduction to statistical concepts for education and behavioral sciences*. Mahwah, NJ: Lawrence Erlbaum Associates. 2001.

Interviewing

Flick, U. *An introduction to qualitative research*. Thousand Oaks, CA: Sage. 1998.

Foddy, W. *Constructing questions for interviews and questionnaires: theory and practice in social research.* New York: Cambridge University Press. 1993.

Survey Design

Babbie, E. *Survey research methods.* Belmont, CA: Wadsworth. 1990.

Cherulnik, P. D. *Methods for behavioral research: a systematic approach.* Thousand Oaks, CA: Sage. 2001.

Konijn, H. S. *Statistical theory of sample survey design and analysis.* New York: Elsevier. 1988.

Index

About the Author

Robert O. Brinkerhoff, Ed.D. is Professor of Counseling Psychology at Western Michigan University, where he coordinates graduate programs in human resources development. He also serves as principal consultant for The Learning Alliance in Portage, Michigan, a firm that provides staff development and consultation in training strategy, effectiveness, and evaluation and is affiliated with Triad, a learning design and development firm in Farmington Hills, Michigan. His prior work experience includes a five-year stint as an officer in the U.S. Navy, a carpenter, charter-boat mate in the West Indies, grocery salesman in Puerto Rico, and factory laborer in Birmingham, England where he saw the original Beatles. He earned a doctorate at the University of Virginia in program evaluation where he also directed the Evaluation Training Consortium, an eleven-year project funded by the U.S. Office of Special Education that provided training in program evaluation to several thousand USOE grantees nationwide.

Rob Brinkerhoff's focus in the past decade has been as an expert in evaluation and training effectiveness. He has provided consultation to dozens of major companies and organizations in the United States, South Africa, Russia, Europe, Australia, New Zealand, Singapore, and Saudi Arabia. Several companies and agencies have adopted his "high impact training" framework, among them The World Bank, QUALCOMM,

Compaq (now Hewlett Packard), State Farm Insurance, Coaching.com, Steelcase, Anheuser Busch, and Whirlpool Corp.

Brinkerhoff is an author of numerous books on evaluation and training, and has been a keynote speaker and presenter at many conferences and institutes worldwide. He has four children, and lives with his wife Stevie and several dogs and other assorted animals in Richland, a small rural village in Southwest Michigan.

He and his colleagues at The Learning Alliance continue to develop the Success Case Method. Together, they provide evaluation services, consultation, and certification training in the SCM through an action learning process. For information about these and other services contact The Learning Alliance at learningalliance@chartermi.net or www.triadperform.com or contact Rob directly at brinkerhoff@wmich.edu.

Berrett-Koehler Publishers

Berrett-Koehler is an independent publisher of books, audios, and other publications at the leading edge of new thinking and innovative practice on work, business, management, leadership, stewardship, career development, human resources, entrepreneurship, and global sustainability.

Since the company's founding in 1992, we have been committed to creating a world that works for all by publishing books, periodicals, and other publications that help us to integrate our values with our work and work lives, and to create more humane and effective organizations.

To find out about our new books, special offers, free excerpts, and much more, subscribe to our **free monthly eNewsletter** at **www.bkconnection.com**.

Please see next pages for other publications
from Berrett-Koehler Publishers

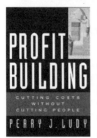

Profit Building
Cutting Costs Without Cutting People

Perry Ludy

Cultivating a loyal, productive workforce is crucial to business success. In *Profit Building,* Perry Ludy—who has worked for top companies in every major field from manufacturing to retail—introduces a five-step process called the PBP (Profit Building Process), which offers specific techniques for improving profitability by stimulating creative thinking and motivating teams to work together more effectively.

Hardcover, 200 pages • ISBN 1-57675-108-2
Item #51082-415 $27.95

Responsible Restructuring
Creative and Profitable Alternatives to Layoffs

Wayne F. Cascio

Responsible Restructuring draws on the results of an eighteen-year study of S&P 500 firms to prove that it makes good business sense to restructure responsibly —to avoid downsizing and instead regard employees as assets to be developed rather than costs to be cut. Cascio offers specific, step-by-step advice on developing and implementing a restructuring strategy that, unlike layoffs, leaves the organization stronger and better able to face the challenges ahead.

Hardcover, 144 pages • ISBN 1-57675-129-5
Item #51295-415 $27.95

Driving Growth Through Innovation
How Leading Firms Are Transforming Their Futures

Robert B. Tucker

Driving Growth Through Innovation offers a practical, comprehensive approach for designing and imple-menting an enterprise-wide innovation strategy. Robert Tucker details numerous case studies of how innovation-adept companies are going beyond the conventional methods of market research, focus groups, and customer surveys to completely retool their ideational processes.

Hardcover, 256 pages • ISBN 1-57675-187-2
Item #51872-415 $27.95

Berrett-Koehler Publishers
PO Box 565, Williston, VT 05495-9900
Call toll-free! **800-929-2929** 7 am-9 pm Eastern Standard Time

Or fax your order to 802-864-7627
For fastest service order online: **www.bkconnection.com**